My Father's Keeper

My Father's Keeper ❧

The Story of a Gay Son and His Aging Parents

Jonathan G. Silin

Beacon Press
Boston

Beacon Press
25 Beacon Street
Boston, Massachusetts 02108-2892
www.beacon.org

Beacon Press books
are published under the auspices of
the Unitarian Universalist Association of Congregations.

09 08 07 06   8 7 6 5 4 3 2 1

This book is printed on acid-free paper that meets the uncoated paper
ANSI/NISO specifications for permanence as revised in 1992.

Composition by Wilsted & Taylor Publishing Services

Library of Congress Cataloging-in-Publication Data

Silin, Jonathan G.
My father's keeper : the story of a gay son and his aging parents / Jonathan G. Silin.
    p. cm.
ISBN 0-8070-7964-2 (hardcover : alk. paper) 1. Adult children of aging parents—
United States—Biography. 2. Caregivers—United States—Biography. 3. Aging
parents—Care—United States. 4. Gay men—United States—Family relationships.
5. Sons—United States—Family relationships. I. Title.

HQ1064.U5S536 2005
306.8740973—dc22   2005030371

Three of the chapters in this book have been published in different forms, including:
"The Future in Question," *Journal of Curriculum Theorizing*; "Reading, Writing, and
the Wrath of My Father," *Reading Research Quarterly*; "My Father, His Psychiatrists,
and Me," *Studies in Gender and Sexuality*.

For my father

Writing books as the highest means of defense
against dangers from inside and outside. . . .
ANNA FREUD

Contents

Prelude   xi

1. New Responsibilities   1

2. Out of Control   13

3. The Future in Question   31

4. Psychic Reality   47

5. Reading, Writing, and the Wrath of My Father   67

6. Unspoken Subjects   91

7. The Other Side of Silence   105

8. My Father, His Psychiatrists, and Me   123

Coda   145

Prelude

> The desire to write is not so much nostalgia for
> the past but a preoccupation with the future.
>
> STEPHEN APPEL, *Psychoanalysis and Pedagogy*

The year I turned fifty I finally understood that my parents were dying. Not all at once, but slowly, by degrees. It was a call to their doctor to remind him about an angiogram that had gone unscheduled for many weeks that brought this truth home to me. I inquired if he had forgotten it. No, he replied, it's just that the priorities had shifted. As the diagnoses mounted—coronary disease, ulcers, cancer, glaucoma—the strategies changed rapidly. Other tests were more urgently needed. New interventions had taken precedence. I found it difficult to keep up with this marathon course of treatments, the American way of death.

My sister-in-law, who studies Buddhist meditation, didn't understand all this frantic activity. She told me it was better to accept the inevitable. In self-defense I told her that I was not trying to extend my parents' lives beyond their "natural" limits, only to contain their deaths. I wanted to hold some of their anxieties and fears for them, to sustain a modicum of practical and emotional order in a chaotic time. I knew my sister-in-law was right, but her advice was diluted by the twelve thousand miles between Hong Kong and Amagansett, New

York, that separated our lives. By then, with a torrent of phone calls to make, forms to fill out, and doctors to see, willy-nilly I was in the middle of a process that seemed to be spinning out of control.

I can only tell the story of my parents' last years from my own perspective. The losses I experienced were mostly psychic, whereas my parents' losses were all too real, including the physical and mental capabilities, the independence and autonomy that characterized their prior lives. At the same time, we shared a rapidly growing familiarity with the world of the frail elderly. Wheelchairs and walkers, ambulettes and guardrails, health aides and therapists of every description became a way of life for all of us.

In the midst of illnesses, agonizing decisions, and the strains of precarious daily lives, we drew closer than we had ever been before. My brother in Asia did his best to appear at times of crisis, but he was neither constitutionally nor practically capable of shouldering the day-to-day burdens of care. My niece, who lived in New York during most of my parents' difficult years, was able to participate in their care for extended periods of time, an undertaking that sorely taxed her previously close relationship with them.

As primary caregiver, most critical for me was the support of my partner, Bob, and the deep connection that he built with my parents. When dispatched to bring my mother home from the hospital, who else but Bob would allow my mother, a lifelong smoker, the illicit pleasure of a cigarette after a month of enforced abstinence. I imagine them just a few feet away from the hospital entrance; my mother knew her etiquette, leaning against the wall of the old limestone and red brick building, chatting casually about the beautiful spring day. Finally discharged, my mother prepared herself to make the first of what would turn into multiple transitions from hospital to home with the help of the addictive substance that was the source of many of her ongoing medical problems. She trusted Bob. Only when she was ready would he insist that she remain safely in place while he searched for a taxi to transport them home.

Three years later, when my father determined to forgo an operation that would potentially prolong his life beyond the three months he might otherwise have—a decision he would inexplicably reverse at the very last minute—who else but Bob could accompany me from his hospital room to my mother's dining room to bring her the news. In bathrobe and slippers, crumbled on the couch, her eyes brimming with tears, my mother was in desperate disbelief. She had opposed my father's decision, which she viewed as an act of personal desertion and unacceptable despair. No matter how he suffered or how debilitated he became, life without my father was unimaginable. For me, playing this new role of intermediary between my parents would have been impossible without Bob's calm demeanor and compassionate heart. While I did most of the explaining, rationalizing, and hand-holding that night, Bob was the frame that held the fraught picture in place. Together we could do what was necessary.

Freud makes clear that the unconscious knows nothing about time and logic. Because I write from both unconscious and conscious sources, my perspective is not chronological. Informed by the emotions and themes that played themselves out over the last decade, the narrative gives short shrift to the real-time sequence of events. I recognize that for some readers a more precise accounting of the facts that gave rise to the stories that follow will offer some assistance in making sense of the often senseless experiences they chronicle.

The central events of the book took my parents from being elderly and independent to being elderly, frail, and completely dependent on others. The first draft of the manuscript was completed more than a year before my father's death in March 2002. The last draft was finished a month before my mother's in May 2005. Because I began writing scraps of narrative at the onset of my parents' decline in 1995, the project bears both the strengths and weaknesses of a lengthy history. In retrospect, it is still easier to know the terminus than the starting point of this narrative. I took on the mantle of caregiver in a slow, incremental process—marked by many bitter battles over domestic control and small poignant moments of mutual recognition—rather than in a few dramatic incidents through which a shift in roles is undeniably inscribed in the book of life.

My parents proved to be tenacious survivors who clung to life until the very end. Although my father had already lost the sight in one eye to glaucoma and the ability to walk safely to severe spinal stenosis by his mid-eighties, it was not till 1997, at age eighty-six, that he was diagnosed with cancer of the larynx, a disease that may recur but that does not generally travel to other parts of the body. His first surgery, a partial laryngectomy, left him with a weak voice and greatly impaired ability to swallow. Within a year, he required the insertion of a gastronomy tube to assure sufficient hydration and food. While not in itself a serious procedure, the insertion of the gastronomy tube precipitated a serious emotional crisis for my father, a realization that even his best efforts at compliance could not overcome the unexpected effects of the initial surgery. Then, a year later, in the winter of 1999, the cancer returned, requiring the removal of his remaining larynx. Ironically, while this intervention brought with it the complete loss of speech, it also restored his ability to swallow. My father could eat and drink again, but his communications were now permanently confined to pen and paper. In the following year, at age eighty-nine, he fell and broke his hip. Although it was repaired without difficulty, because of his greatly reduced mobility it was no longer possible to organize care at home. He was forced to take up permanent residence in the nursing home where he had gone for rehabilitation and where he died two years later.

The story of my mother's decline begins in 1995, at age eighty-three, when an ulcer threatened to break through the lining of her stomach and cause imminent death from peritonitis. A prolonged hospitalization left her severely depressed and unable to take care of my father. Three years later, in the summer of 1998, as she was preparing to celebrate her sixty-second wedding anniversary, she fell and broke her hip. Despite being confined to a walker and suffering frequent, less-damaging falls, numerous small strokes, heart problems, and an addiction to cigarettes that continued through her very last bout with pneumonia, my mother lived for two years after my father and died in May 2005 at age ninety-two.

At different places in my telling of this story different aspects of my perspective take prominence over others. Just as this is not a chronological telling, so the identities from which I write are never isolated but always overlapping and interacting. Most obviously I am the middle-aged son caring for his parents, trying first to discern and then honor their wishes. At the same time I am the gay man who becomes the emotional and practical center of his heterosexual family. My history as an outsider and black sheep, along with my experiences caring for people with HIV/AIDS, informs the story as much as my profession—early childhood educator.

In truth, I am more practiced in writing scholarly essays than in recording personal events. My understanding of the value of storytelling, however, is rooted in my life as a gay man and educator. As someone who has benefited from the movements for social change in the 1960s and '70s, I am primed to look with a critical eye at traditional forms of science and to listen for stories that go against the grain. I know from firsthand experience that psychiatrists and psychologists once routinely passed wrongful judgments on lesbians and gay men. I know too that traditional theories of child development often functioned to normalize some children and families while pathologizing others. I have learned to value first-person narratives for the compelling ways they can testify to the emotional truths of our lives.

Documenting my parents' final decade highlighted the fluid movement between my personal and professional lives. I found myself, for example, teaching my graduate education students about lifespan development rather than focusing on the early years, when changes are more rapid and obvious. I wanted my students to think about how child-parent relationships evolve over time and to provide frequent opportunities for them to rethink the past through narrative writing.

Even as my teaching changed, I was surprised to realize how frequently I used my professional knowledge with my parents. Familiarity with Montessori methods, for example, informed the way that I carefully parsed apart the simplest tasks. Two weeks prior to Thanksgiving, I began to hear my mother's worries about organizing the annual Christmas gifts for the apartment building employees. Like cooking with children in the classroom, I knew the importance of having all the materials—crisp, new ten-dollar bills, cards, envelopes, stamps, pens, and list of employees—arranged in advance. I also knew the importance of routines. Over and over again I repeated the new schedule for the health aides. As if preparing for the departure of a much-loved student teacher from the kindergarten, I carefully calculated the amount of warning that my parents needed before making changes in household help. Like my students, I wanted my parents to have sufficient time for processing the information and achieving emotional closure, but not so much time that they experienced the disabling fears that could be precipitated by alterations in their domestic arrangements.

Despite my reliance on early childhood skills, I did not see my mother and father as children. No matter how dependent they became, they were still my parents. Our history was not erased by their changed circumstances, no matter how often I was called upon to contain their feelings of loss and anxiety. I tried to perform the role of reassuring presence in their life. Just as I learned during the first fire drills of each school year to say with a calm authority to the apprehensive four-year-olds by my side, "I will make sure that nothing happens to you. I will take care of you," so I learned to talk with my mother about her upcoming cataract surgery and to my father about the replacement of his gastronomy tube. But to imagine that our roles were reversed would have undermined their dignity while burdening me with confusing emotions.

In his book *In the American West,* the photographer Richard Avedon said of his work, "A portrait is not a likeness. The moment an emotion or fact is transformed into a photograph, it is no longer a fact but an opinion. There is no such thing as inaccuracy in a photograph. All photographs are accurate. None of them is the truth." In the end, it is my telling of our family story that is recorded here. I have tried to situate this telling in the idiosyncrasies of my perspective. There are certainly other perspectives from which the story might have been written, and there are other authors in my family who may one day choose to do just that. For the moment, I can only hope that my parents would feel that their final years have been well told, and their experiences imbued with meanings not too terribly distant from ones that they would recognize, if not necessarily claim as their own.

I

New Responsibilities

> If you want to endure life, prepare for death.
>
> SIGMUND FREUD, "Thoughts for
> the Times on War and Death"

We are in the lawyer's office. My father walks with a metal cane with four prongs at the bottom to steady himself. The combination of spinal disease and partial loss of sight makes his balance precarious. My mother, dressed in a Depression-era brown suit, raincoat, and hat to match, still moves quickly and independently. She is forever pressing ahead of my father, seemingly unaware of how slowly he moves. The stomach surgery and torn knee ligaments that will soon impede her mobility have not yet taken their toll. She clutches a manila envelope. We are here at my insistence to review the legal documents—wills, powers of attorney, living wills—that are designed to ensure a measure of control over the uncertainties that inevitably surround illness and death.

I am beginning to feel the weight of new responsibilities. But I am totally unprepared for what I hear, and don't hear, once we are installed in the glass-walled conference room. We sit at the far end of a long table, my mother and father next to each other on one side and

I on the other. When Mr. Halperin enters, he sits at the head of the table, between us, in the negotiator's position. A short, slightly over-weight, solid-looking burgher in dark blue suit, this man of affairs is considerably younger than I. I am sharply conscious of my own age, fifty-one at the time, and wonder if my parents' fragile appearance somehow makes me look even older. He talks easily and with confidence. I am reassured. Despite my parents' resistance, I have done the right thing bringing them here.

My father speaks slowly and deliberately as he provides the demographic information requested, including details about my brother and his wife and child. When he finishes, there is a long silence. Something is wrong. My heart is pounding, my hands are shaking, and adrenaline is coursing through my body. Then, overcoming a deep sense of terror, emboldened by a mix of anger, defiance, and urgency, I speak the unspeakable. I announce that I too live with someone. I too am an adult with a life partner who cannot be expunged from the record. Without hesitation, Mr. Halperin turns to me and notes the information I provide about Bob, my partner of twenty-five years. When I finally look up at my parents, their faces register shock and distress. They say nothing.

It can't be the information I convey that leaves my parents silent. After all, I have been openly gay for decades, Bob regularly attends family functions, and they actually seem to like him. No, it is my insistence that Bob be written into the official story of our family that upsets my parents so deeply. In more generous moments, I think about how difficult it must be for my conventional, middle-class parents to speak about a gay relationship. In some ways their vocabulary has not caught up with their behavior. In other ways their cordial but emotionally distant relationship with Bob is not unlike their relationship with my brother's wife. Although she is an officially documented member of the family, she is not mentioned in their wills. My brother and I are to receive income from a trust, and upon our deaths the money will go to my niece.

Mr. Halperin, a specialist in elder care, quickly declares my parents' plan inadvisable; the small size of the estate would provide little income and be quickly consumed by bank fees. Later, when I point out the inequity of the arrangement since I don't have children, my parents express outrage at the idea that someone who is not a blood relative might ultimately inherit their money. Mr. Halperin ends the meeting with a description of the financial risks that my parents incur by retaining direct control over their resources should they require prolonged hospitalization or care at a nursing home. He advises them to place their money in a Medicare trust immediately.

We leave the meeting dazed. I because of the emotional energy required to assert Bob's place in the family, and my parents because they are forced to confront the inadequacy of their carefully wrought plans. Implicit too is the message that their youngest son, the rebel of the family who is not supposed to care about material matters, has taken the lead in developing a practical strategy for the future. Suddenly the ground has shifted. We are crossing a border into another country, the country of the frail elderly.

Although my parents are yet to suffer the multiple medical crises that will bring us to the heart of this new territory, a subtle psychological shift begins in Mr. Halperin's conference room. It's been a long and difficult passage from the time when my parents were newly retired and still independent to the present, when they are reliant on a cornucopia of medications and round-the-clock health aides to get through the day. In the beginning, neither they nor I knew where we were going, or even that we were in the midst of a journey. We were reluctant travelers who would have preferred to stay just where we had been during the prior decades. But within two years, a series of life-threatening illnesses rapidly propelled us forward into the domain of the frail elderly. We were each in our own way still struggling to understand the changed situation and our radically altered relationship.

After our meeting with Mr. Halperin that afternoon, I place my parents in a taxi and head for the subway. At Bank Street College, where I teach teachers, there will surely be sympathetic listeners for the drama that has just played itself out. Although the degree of direct involvement differs, everyone has a story to tell about aging parents. While we once talked about students, proposed changes in the curriculum, and our visits to local schools as we waited to use the copy machine, now my colleagues and I are more often overheard discussing the merits of various nursing homes, health aides, and geriatricians. Like my immediate peers, I find it difficult to establish the right distance from my parents. At times I am envious of my older brother, who has lived in Asia since his graduate school days and long ago established the geographic and emotional space that characterizes his response to their needs. As I struggle to maintain practical and psychological boundaries when assisting my parents, time becomes blurred. Even as my new role evokes memories of childhood, I am forced to abandon images of my parents as omniscient and invulnerable and myself as the one in need of care and protection. I am forever a child—even as I have become the decision maker and emotional center of the family.

In the beginning of my parents' decline, I spent a great deal of time testing the present against what I remembered of the past, mourning my lost youth and the parents who were part of it. It seemed the only way to make sense of what was happening, of the radically changed relationship we had entered. My memories were hazy, and aspects of my parents I hadn't seen before disoriented me. I had a sense of loss at the same time as I wasn't quite clear about what I had given up. Was my father cantankerous and depressed or socially skilled and ambitious? Was my mother confident and extremely capable or shy and riddled with self-doubt? How could I reconcile the disparate images of now and then, of them and me?

Because I am an early childhood educator, I have many opportunities to think about the life cycle in more disciplined, less emotionally laden ways—observation in classrooms, work with teachers, and study of the scientific literature that describes human development. Spending so much time with my parents, I find that I am not only revisiting my own past but also the very idea of childhood. The assumption that childhood is a long-ago event—one that is portrayed in popular books as leaving us either with scars that never completely heal or with deep nostalgia for an idyllic time that can never be recovered—no longer seems certain. The memories, relationships, and ways of knowing I thought I had abandoned years ago are still a dynamic part of the present. Perhaps development works through addition rather than substitution, with our new skills and insights joining rather than replacing old ones. Perhaps childhood is less a foundational moment fixed in the distant past than an open book that can be edited and reinterpreted over time.

In class the night after the meeting with Mr. Halperin, my parents' lawyer, we discuss Amy Tan's *The Joy Luck Club*. My niece, Anne, who grew up in Hong Kong and whose mother is Taiwanese, tells me that it is a book filled with stereotypes and that misrepresents Chinese culture. Nevertheless, I am still drawn to its central theme of loss and reconciliation, unashamedly moved by its sentimentality and descriptions of intergenerational conflict. When the book's protagonist, June Woo, resists the suggestion of the club that she travel to China to tell her half-sisters about her mother's death—"What will I say? What can I tell them about my mother? I don't know anything. She was my mother"—I feel the truth of her words in the pit of my stomach. In the class, I talk about the ineffable mysteries that often surround the people whom we know most intimately, as if our very closeness prevents us from seeing and appreciating the whole. Images from the afternoon fill my head. How do my parents understand this last period of their lives? What do they make of my efforts to help them organize their affairs? Why are they so reluctant to trust me?

Further on in the book, when another middle-aged daughter gains enough distance to recognize that her mother is no longer the formidable enemy she once imagined—"I could finally see what was really there: an old woman, a wok for her armor, a knitting needle for her sword, getting a little crabby as she waited patiently for her daughter to invite her in"—I think about being caught up in power struggles with my parents, struggles I presumed long over. We argue over everything from household help and an appointment with the heart specialist to the purchase of a hearing aid and an application for a bank card. The frustration of trying to help two fiercely independent people sometimes causes me to lose all perspective and patience.

I am drawn back to the classroom by my twenty-something students, all women, who resonate with the stories of mother-daughter conflict in Tan's book but complain that they have trouble telling the characters apart. They blame the author for failing to draw distinguishing psychological portraits of the mothers and daughters. I talk about cultural differences and the Western emphasis on the individual, and about the differences between novels, such as Amy Tan's, in which the characters are defined by how they act or fail to act and novels that are predicated on extended exploration of their protagonists' interior lives. I even manage to speak about some of the cultural myths to which my niece had alerted me. Afterward, however, as the students gather up their notebooks, half-eaten sandwiches, and containers of cold soup and coffee, I am left to gather together the emotional fragments of my own day.

During class I have tried to fend off thoughts of my aging parents even as I wonder if there are any larger lessons in their story for the students. Despite my parents' growing fears and vulnerabilities, they are not childlike in any way. Nor do they give any indication that they expect or would like to be cared for. We have begun a complex dance in which I am learning to offer assistance, and they are learning to accept their new limitations. Never an accomplished dancer, I stumble frequently as I try to master new steps. I wonder about who is leading and who is following and find that I must listen carefully, for the music changes daily. Sometimes it is slow and sweet as we remember the past together, sometimes it is fast and staccato as we are pressed to make critical healthcare decisions. At other moments it seems that we are all on the same dance floor moving to different tunes.

This dance brings to the fore painful memories of my parents' frequent and intrusive interventions into my own life. Hovering over me as a child, they sought to read every emotional undercurrent for indications of restless waters, muddied streams, and paralyzing logjams. While they celebrated my most minor achievements with pride, they also did not hesitate to secure professional assistance in the form of tutors and counselors if academic or emotional progress was in doubt. When I was in the throes of an adolescent identity crisis, struggling to manage my first gay love affairs, my mother's letter to the psychiatrist requesting information about my treatment seemed unforgivable to me. The fact that she was a former mental health professional made my outrage at her failure to respect the confidential nature of the therapeutic relationship all the more bitter.

Now I have become the intrusive one, no longer trusting my parents to provide accurate reports of their medical interviews. Some time ago, I timidly asked my father's permission to call his doctor. I was taken aback by his response, "Of course. You *should* call. You're my son." I immediately reproached myself for having waited too long to do what sons *should* do. On reflection, I understood his reply not as a rebuke but as an invitation to become more actively involved in his care. My father was instructing me about what he expects and needs.

My mother too has ideas about what a son should do, although they are not about speaking to others, but about how to communicate in a crisis. These instructions were delivered from her bed in the intensive care unit of the hospital, on the day following the surgery to repair an ulcer that had burst through the lining of her stomach, when peritonitis threatened her life. My mother's speech was slurred, the lingering effects of multiple painkillers, but her presence of mind was unshaken. She lay immobile, tubes of every description leading into and out of her body. When I entered the room, I immediately took her hand. Naturally shy and undemonstrative, I have been taught by HIV/AIDS the necessity of overcoming this reticence. Just as quickly, my mother asked, "Is your hand shaking?" My mother had not been given to straight talk in the past, and I was taken aback. Her words seemed out of character. "No," I lied in response to her query as she went on sternly, "Because I don't need that." My mother was clearly telling me what she needed, and I tried to provide the strength she was asking for. Later, when my father tried to tease her about getting better so that she could look after him, the expression on her face told me that she wasn't amused. She wanted only to be cared for, intolerant at the moment of anyone else's weaknesses.

Sometimes my parents' instructions were less direct and more subtle, as on the day we were squeezed into the booth of a coffee shop not far from the apartment that my father's eldest sister had lived in for many years. Nearly ninety, she had moved into a nearby nursing home. It was an unusual event for us to be eating lunch together, but then so was the occasion, a respite from sorting through the contents of her soon-to-be-relinquished apartment. My father cleaned his hands with a Wash'n Dri towelette, one of the great modern conveniences for someone phobic about germs and eating in unfamiliar places. After some talk about the remaining tasks—securing a reputable antiques appraiser, the difficulties of arranging the Salvation Army pickup, the appropriate order in which various family members might stake their claims on cherished objects—I cleared a space for my own impatient query. Why had it taken two years to let go of the apartment? I wanted to know. How could they rationalize paying so much rent for so long on an unoccupied apartment? By then my father was eating his tuna fish directly from the single-serving-size can so as to avoid the unsanitary procedure of picking up a sandwich. My mother pecked, birdlike, at her food. They were both clearly uncomfortable with my line of questioning. My father frowned and remained silent. "Far too much to eat," my mother evasively exclaimed, as if overwhelmed by the untidy aesthetics of the egg salad that oozed from between the slices of rye bread. Finally, my father ventured that he had been waiting for the right moment. I pressed forward. How did he know that she was ready now? A man who usually enjoyed a large vocabulary and the hunt for the perfect words to describe a person or event, my father was suddenly and surprisingly inarticulate. He resisted my probes, as if I had asked an embarrassingly personal question. He acknowledged that although he knew that giving up the apartment was inevitable, he had had no idea when that moment would come. In the last several months, however, my aunt had made no references to her former home or possessions. It was not that she had forgotten the apartment so much as that it had disappeared from her immediate view. She was ensconced in the nursing home routines and knew no other life.

Although everything that my father said made sense, I found myself dissatisfied with his explanation and the reluctant way in which it was proffered. I knew my father was a kind and thoughtful person; after all, he had even arranged for my aunt to make one last visit to the apartment before it was dismantled. And several weeks later, I was impressed by the controlled and generous way my aunt talked about the furniture that I had taken from her apartment—the dining room table that now sits neatly against the wall in the small house in which Bob and I have lived for so long and that miraculously expands to accommodate twelve for our frequent holiday dinners, the two darkly lacquered and vaguely oriental side chairs that provide our otherwise ordinary living room with a touch of elegance, the little black chest of drawers that so conveniently contains our wills and other important papers. Yet it took several years for me to appreciate the wisdom of my father's judgment. I came to understand how important the passage of time could be in helping my parents themselves adjust to previously unacceptable conditions, to the loss of control over their bodies and of the independence they cherished. I saw how being consumed with getting through the present could trump nostalgia for the past, and how a preoccupation with what has been lost can be curtailed by an attentive gesture in the moment.

As an educator, I should not have been surprised that the instruction my parents offered in the coffee shop required several years to take hold. I am supposed to know about the complex ways that teaching and learning occurs, about the difficulties of separation from loved ones and the comforting, transitional objects that contain our sadness and our memories. After all, beginnings and endings aren't so very different. They are times in our lives when autonomy and dependency, desire and self-sufficiency, affiliation and separation are experienced in heightened forms.

Despite these many parallels, my knowledge of early childhood is far more complete than my knowledge of old age, my educator voice far more certain than my eldercare skills. I have only to recall my increasingly frequent and anxious visits with my parents when I was still overwhelmed by their problems and my own desire to fix them. I fretted uselessly about their apartment that suffered from decades of neglect. I saw carpets worn black with dirt, chairs lumpy with broken springs, lamps covered with torn shades. I desperately wanted these things to matter to my parents—but they didn't. I tried to organize the kitchen counters littered with dozens of pillboxes, bottles of cough syrup, and warnings about the dangers of the very drugs keeping them alive. As we talked of symptoms and treatment options, I feverishly sorted through piles of unopened mail, stacks of unread magazines, accumulations of unused coupons. I wanted to create order out of the confusion brought on by so much illness.

When I come to visit, it always seems that I am leaving too soon. There is never enough time. When I arrive, I focus on my mother, whose first question is about the length of my stay and the bus that I will take home. Although she continues to glance anxiously at her watch throughout the visit, the conversation shifts to the events of my week. Always the great escape artist, eager to pretend that everything is okay and to find relief from her own difficulties in other people's lives, she does not want to talk about herself and the endless round of doctors' appointments that mark her days. From a distance, I understand that for my mother, denial has been an effective survival strategy. Up close, I experience impatience, sometimes anger. It is often impossible to determine problems in need of attention and hard to always fill the void left by her lack of self-representation with diverting stories from my own life.

After attending to my mother, I turn to my father, knowing that neither he nor I will be satisfied with the evening's accomplishments. It's not for lack of planning, but in his late eighties he tires easily and has difficulty staying focused. I try to set out a short agenda. I wait till we have settled in a bit. When he is especially fatigued or withdrawn, this entails a silent sitting together. If he is outgoing and energetic, he reports the latest crisis precipitated by a misplaced bill or a government form in need of completion. Experience teaches me that any one of these tales of loss and recovery can take over the entire evening. I listen with care but don't ask too many questions.

Given my father's desire to take an active part in managing his own affairs and my commitment to a collaborative effort, I soon venture my own list of concerns, the product of a week's deliberation. While my father is often caught up in the most immediate events—making sure that the rent is paid no later than the tenth of the month or that his taxes are posted by April 15—my interests might best be classified as midrange—bringing some order to the Byzantine banking arrangements that make it impossible to keep accurate records or setting up a visit to a psychiatrist to adjust the antidepressant drugs that no longer seem effective. Our concerns are different. Although my father has demonstrated every determination to live through several medical catastrophes, he grows impatient and angry with discussions about the future. I, on the other hand, who did not know a treasury note from a junk bond just a few years ago, now wake up at night obsessed with the latest interest rates and best forms of investment. Thinking that one or both of my parents may live into their nineties, I want us to be prepared as best we can.

By the end of the visit, we have negotiated a program that includes one issue from his list and one from mine. We are both exhausted and cranky. Perhaps he is right anyway; better to stay in the moment than worry about an unpredictable future. Needing to catch my bus, I know I haven't stayed long enough. How could it ever be enough?

Part of me leaves my parents as an adult leaves a young child on the first day of school, wondering if she can really make it on her own. Will the home health aide be up to the task of caring for my parents?

Will they behave or will some sudden outburst cause her to quit? Another part of me leaves as a child leaves a parent, ambivalent about my ability to survive without them. Infirmities aside, my parents still provide a slim barrier against my mortality. At the same time, I imagine the relief I will feel when they are dead. These guilty thoughts are only tempered by sadness at their severely diminished capacities.

2

Out of Control

> To tolerate life remains, after all,
> the first duty of all living beings.
> SIGMUND FREUD, "Thoughts for
> the Times on War and Death"

The clock on the newly installed electronic signboard looks official, almost believable. It reads 3:04, the precise moment my train is supposed to arrive. I am outside, on platform number one of Newark's Penn Station, avoiding the damp waiting area with its musty smells and crowded benches. Leaning over the track, peering ahead, seeing no movement of any kind, I calculate the chances—fifty-fifty—of completing a phone call before the train pulls in. It is a courtesy call to my parents—"Okay if I stop by?" I will ask politely—knowing full well there is nothing they can say that will stop me.

It's been a better than usual day. The Jefferson Avenue School has a large cluster of teachers working with the major urban school-reform project for which a colleague and I serve as the researchers/evaluators. The principal has even provided us with a small office, and I don't have to ask for the key to the men's room, as I do at our ten other sites. The office is crammed with old metal filing cabinets, desks, and storage boxes belonging to a previous reform effort that has long since been disbanded. But it's a good place to hang a coat, store a backpack, and seek a few minutes respite from a round of classroom observations.

Inevitably I come away from these visits impressed by the struggle of the teachers to meet the many needs of their students who are growing up in severely decaying neighborhoods. The teachers must also circumvent the multiple obstacles placed in their paths by the district bureaucracy. Everywhere I see reams of meaningless paperwork, including elaborate lesson plans without relevance to the children's lives and individual education plans for learning disabled students without resources to implement them. The teachers' desks are piled high with batteries of standardized tests and guidebooks to new reading and math programs that will be deployed in their understaffed and overpopulated classrooms. A calendar distributed by the district displays eight different diagnostic tests that must be administered a total of twenty-one times between September and June in the kindergarten. Some tests are given several times a year and others require the teacher to sit with each child for ten uninterrupted minutes, no mean feat for even the most well-organized teacher alone in a room with twenty-three five-year-olds.

Images from the day—Catherine's extraordinary conversation with her kindergartners, Stephanie's calm control of her second grade, and the chaos of Diane's first grade—fill my head as I reach for the phone, awkwardly crouch down to the key pad, and begin the laborious task of punching in the twenty-three digits required by my credit card call. As I wait, listening to the ringing of the phone and for the sound of an approaching train, I wonder who will answer. While my mother was once guardian of the phone and monitor of all worldly contact, my father has just begun to usurp this function. An important practical and symbolic shift indicating his renewed interest in social life, it is testimony to the workings of a powerful new drug cocktail—an antipsychotic to reduce agitation, a tranquilizer to intensify its effects, and a mood stabilizer to prevent sudden outbursts of anger.

I am, however, unprepared for the emotion in my father's voice when he finally answers the phone. "It's been two days since we've heard from you. I was terribly worried. I thought something had happened to you." In a hurry, but wanting to acknowledge his concern, I remind him that my days in the field are very busy and that I am on my way to see him now. He is immediately relieved, and there is nothing more for me to say. Later that night I will play back two messages on my home answering machine and two more on my office voice mail. All are in the same plaintive, raspy, hardly audible voice, "Jonathan, this is your father. Where are you? I'm worried."

Despite these words of concern, when I settle into my seat for the brief ride to the city, I am apprehensive about my visit. I wonder if the sudden attacks, which have greeted me throughout the preceding year, are over. Will there really be no battles over money or arguments about the qualifications of his health aides? I am not yet trusting of the new drugs, although there have been other indications of their positive effects. Just this Saturday my father called early in the morning to say that he had been awake all night deciding to give up his obsessive attempts to redeem some very old and very worthless insurance policies. He did not admit that his calculations have been wrong or that the company's are right. What he did say is that the policies are not worth fighting about and that he would be happier doing other things. I didn't want to say anything to give him second thoughts. I told him it was a good decision because it's too exhausting to fight all the time. When I asked him why he was ending a four-month battle that has consumed his every waking hour, he said that sooner or later, "the family" will get the money. I have learned enough in these years not to contradict him by insisting on the truth.

The real test of the medications came the same afternoon, when my father called again to ask why I hadn't sold the insurance policy, as he had directed me to do. I summoned up my best early childhood education skills, walked him through our earlier conversation, and patiently waited for his acknowledgment at the end of each statement. "Remember when you called this morning?"

"Yes."

"And you said you had been up all night thinking about the insurance policies?"

"Yes."

"And you said that you were tired of fighting with everyone about them?"

"Yes."

"And you said we would get the money in the end?"

"Yes." Finally he seemed to remember the first decision and to be reassured that it was the correct one. I was unnerved by this need for a step-by-step rehearsal, glad to have found the right strategy this time, and concerned about my ability to find the appropriate tone on future occasions.

Calm and composed, my parents seem genuinely glad to see me when I arrive at their apartment. After a few minutes of family news and recent doctor reports, I find myself listening as my father describes his daily schedule. I don't know how this recitation begins and why it is taking place, but I try to follow it with interest. Then suddenly, without any warning, somewhere in midmorning after the opening routines of the day and the regular phone conversation with my brother in Taipei, my father hits a brick wall. He bursts into inconsolable tears, overcome, as he soon admits, by what he sees as the emptiness of his life. Wanting to comfort him but also to understand what is happening, I wonder out loud why he has become upset at this particular moment. "It's only when I describe my life to you that it seems so bare. Only then do I remember what I once was, only then do I feel despair at what I have become." Suddenly, I am the mirror, the person who forces him to look at his life, and the one who is blamed for what he sees.

My father goes on to inventory the two things that make his life bearable, that provide some reason for going forward—my mother's presence and my brother's phone calls. I am thrilled that he names my mother first, and he even turns to look at her as he speaks. Over the last two years he has found continuous fault with her efforts to care for him. The sweater she offers him is too light or too heavy, the water she brings to soothe his radiation-scarred throat is inevitably too warm or too cold, and her attempts to reach the doctor, too frequent or not frequent enough, seem only to occur at the wrong time of day. Harsh and overbearing, he sees her as the cause of his suffering. If she were dead, he has said, he would not feel obligated to go on living. But for the moment, my mother beams with his approval.

I am also pleased that my father receives such satisfaction from his conversations with my brother about investment strategies. He even manages a smile through his tears when he concedes that my brother is getting pretty good at the stock market. Here he permits himself a moment of real pride even as he declares the work unfinished, thus certifying his ongoing importance as paternal mentor.

Now, as the tone is less somber, I take the ultimate plunge into the icy waters of self-affirmation. "And what about me?" I ask.

"You … " my father stumbles, embarrassed, caught by my directness. "You I don't talk to that much." I am momentarily silenced by this willful lapse of memory.

"Come on," I cajole, "I can't always answer your calls immediately, but we do speak at least once or twice a day." I don't mention the hours of calls I make each week to insure that the health aides are always present, that the doctors are speaking to each other, and that the needs of the accountant, banker, and lawyer are satisfied. In short, I defend myself without feeling at all defensive.

Curious and interested in my father's feelings but experiencing neither anger nor offense, I am not drawn into the emotional maelstrom he creates as he continues to weep. I am baffled by the suddenness with which the storm has hit. Then, the words welling up from deep inside him, a new wave breaks as I hear my father say, "I feel so terrible about the way I have treated you. The way I have fought with you all the time." I am taken aback and wonder if it was my own question that elicited this admission. But just as I felt no anger at my absence from his earlier thoughts, I feel no vindication in my new presence. Mostly, I am sad for him and worried for myself, fearing that he won't be able to regain control of his emotions. When I point out that conflict has been part of our history but that over the last month we haven't had any disagreements, my father cuts to the heart of the matter. "Yes, I know all that. But I guess it's my subconscious that is troubling me. I have been so unfair to you."

Now I understand his earlier concerns for my whereabouts in a new way, as an indicator of his own deep turmoil. While his subconscious is bubbling to the surface, it is being filtered through the screen of a demanding superego that will not let his bad behavior go unpunished. But once these admissions of guilt are in place, no actual apology offered, the therapeutic power of self-expression begins to take over and slowly my father recovers his equanimity. His turbulent emotions are momentarily at rest.

As I prepare to leave, my mother says sotto voce, "I have never seen your father upset like that before." When I remind her of the October incident when he railed against my lack of respect and his loss of control over his affairs, she cannot recall it. When I note that he does not name me among the things that make his daily life worth living, she says that I have misheard him. My mother only recognizes his admission of wrongdoing and hopes that it will erase all traces of prior conflict. She desperately wants me to feel loved and that in return I will continue to love my father despite his thankless behavior. She speaks as his advocate and out of her own self-interest, for she fears that I may abandon them if I feel abandoned by them.

And what are my own interests in these encounters? I am learning not to get on the emotional roller coaster ride that used to make me sick from the sudden heights and death-defying plunges my father engineered. Watching from the ground, I preserve my own mental health. I am a better caregiver, more energetic and clearly focused. At the same time I worry that when I sit out the rides, coolly professional and in control, I have indeed abandoned him in some way, no longer taking his worries seriously. And despite my best efforts to separate and distance myself, can I ever be impermeable to the emotional assaults visited upon me by my parents?

My struggles to become a responsive and caring child to my elderly parents often bring me back to the urban classrooms I visit during the day. I think about the many teachers I have observed who spend much of their time seeking to control their students through a combination of angry outbursts and displays of genuine affection. Larger-than-life maternal figures, they pride themselves on their ability to change the daily schedule on a dime in order to respond to the children's interests. Good cop and bad cop rolled into one, these are charismatic women who appear to teach through the force of personality rather than structuring routines, designing physical space, and developing a curriculum that supports student autonomy.

I think too about the constant surveillance that children are subjected to—not dissimilar to the paternalistic supervision teachers receive from administrators and the school district itself experiences from the state—and of the round-the-clock health aides who stand guard over my parents. Unlike the children, however, my parents are able to articulate their feeling of being held prisoner in their own home. They are indignant when I question plans that will leave them alone for several hours on the day when a health aide must be late for work or that will send my mother to the eye doctor appointment on her own. Don't I think they can manage without her? How hard is it to get a taxi?

In a frequently referenced book, *Discipline and Punish*, Michel Foucault describes the introduction of the Panopticon, a tower that enables a single guard to survey all prison inmates at once, as emblematic of the intensification of technologies of social control in the nineteenth century. I prefer to reflect on the following scene, which I witnessed at the Jefferson Avenue School, for insight about our continuing obsession with controlling the bodies of young children.

Erica, a young and enthusiastic kindergarten teacher, wants to implement a more progressive curriculum but knows that she will be judged by the year-end test scores of her five-year-olds. The first hour of the day is devoted to a review of the schedule, calendar, weather chart, and morning message that is designed to reinforce basic reading and math skills. Erica takes the children through these exercises with the exaggerated zest of a cheerleader. Unfortunately, the routine is as exhausting as it is exhaustive. At 9:50 the squirming group is lined up, the boys on one side of the door and the girls on the other. Quieting the children with an organizing song, Erica prepares to lead them down the cavernous hallway, lined with gigantic silver radiators and musty pink walls, to the main lobby and school bathrooms. During past visits, I have stayed behind in order to catch up on my note taking. My impulse to follow the group this time does not go unnoticed by Hector. "You coming with us, Jonathan?" he asks. I answer in the affirmative but hope that he doesn't probe further. After all, my usual refrain, "I like to see what you are doing and how you learn in school," just doesn't seem appropriate to this activity.

Arriving at our destination as another group is about to leave, Erica props open the heavy wooden doors to the bathrooms and stations herself between them. As the children are called two at a time to enter, she hands each one several pieces of toilet paper from the roll she has brought from the classroom. After everyone has had a turn— no one demurs, though the waiting children are restless, fidgeting with each other's hair and clothing—the next group can be seen entering the lobby.

As we return to the classroom, I suddenly recall a similar ritual, one that I have only read about but that resonates with my own gay history. In A Restricted Country, Joan Nestle describes the all-important bathroom lines in Mafia-owned lesbian bars of the 1950s. Here the door monitor allowed only one person in at a time for fear that salacious interactions might occur if two women entered together. The line, emblematic of the policing of lesbian desire, is also a site for cruising, joking, bantering with the door monitor, and ultimately for resistance. The lines of children I observe are not so very different. They are about containing the bodies of those who are assumed to be potentially out of control, about supervising basic functions, and insuring that peer interaction is always open to surveillance.

My experiences as a gay man growing up and coming out before the Stonewall Riots, the woman who lived restricted and judged on the bathroom line, and the children who live regimented lives in institutions, all attest to the way that vulnerable populations in our culture are closely watched even as they engage in small moments of resistance. Little wonder, then, that I bring particular sensitivities to the complaints of my middle-class parents about the new forms of surveillance they are subject to in their declining years. Indeed, it was in the tiled bathroom designed for younger, more able-bodied people that my father had a serious fall in 2000, despite the fact that his health aide was with him. She turned her back for only a moment to reach for his eye drops and he collapsed. The broken hip was either the result or the cause of the fall. No one knows for sure, or really cares. The surveillance is always imperfect, something every good teacher acknowledges, something every good health aide fears.

The best of the educators that I observe, like the best of the health aides, teach me that care is often delivered through thoughtful reserve and a balanced respect for the emotional needs and physical safety of those who depend upon them.

Catherine is one of these remarkable teachers. When I reach her classroom at 10:15 AM, she is sitting on the floor in a large circle with her group of twenty-seven anxious five-year-olds. Upon arrival at school, the children have learned that a teacher in the next room will be late because of car problems. Subsequently, Catherine has overheard them theorizing about an explosion in the car and life-threatening injuries to Ms. Lewis. Six months pregnant, Catherine awkwardly shifts her body weight in an attempt to find a comfortable position, as she patiently walks through the steps of Ms. Lewis's morning, from leaving her house and trying to start the car, to calling the repair service and notifying the school that she will be late. No matter how many times Catherine reassures them, many children persist in their belief that a major catastrophe has occurred. Frustrated by the worried looks on the children's faces, she calls on her assistant for help. The assistant draws an analogy between the sluggish car unable to start on the cold winter morning and a sleepy child who is reluctant to get out of bed for school. The children are impervious to the charm of this explanation that only seems to add to their confusion.

As I watch this group of young children try to make sense of the morning's events, I am reminded of the conversation with my father on the previous Saturday afternoon about his life insurance. Like my father, the children need everything spelled out. The story must be specific, concrete, and without sidebars. It must be repeated over and over. I am envious of the way Catherine attends both to the quality of her practical explanations and to the underlying fears that are preventing the children from hearing them. It's not the specific issue of Ms. Lewis's car that is important. After all, they could be discussing Chantal's move to a new apartment, the birth of Ba-shey's new baby brother, or the death of Fluffy, the classroom guinea pig. Rather, it is the threats to our survival, posed by dangers both internal and external, that drive their unquenchable anxieties. The children are exquisitely attuned to the potential separations, losses, or displacements in the stories they hear and the events they experience themselves.

Catherine listens to the children with intensity, her insistence that everyone who desires may speak signaling her respect for their concerns. It is the same way I want to hear my father's questions, without succumbing to the anxieties that fuel his interactions with me. Like Catherine, I want to respond to specific concerns as well as to the emotional undercurrents that flow beneath the surface. A literary theorist might say that we need to attend to both the *fabula*, or timeless plight—human jealousy, thwarted ambition—and to the *sjuzet*, or particular plot in which it is embedded. A kind of double consciousness is required at all times.

Catherine also knows when she has hit a wall and new strategies are needed. After a final round of speakers and with signs of lingering uncertainty among them, she announces the end of the conversation. At the same time, she promises to invite Ms. Lewis to join the group in the afternoon to tell the story in her own words and reassure the children that she is unharmed. The kindergartners are then asked to refocus their attention on a short reading lesson before going off to work on their own. There are plenty of blocks, a large dramatic play area, and art materials should they want to rehearse the car difficulties during the course of the morning.

It feels more challenging to absorb and then redirect my parents' anxieties. I wish that they too had access to vehicles other than language to express their feelings and to represent their ideas. Catherine, nevertheless, models a willingness to listen, a firmness when the conversation has reached an end, and an invitation to continue it at another time that I will not forget.

Stephanie is another teacher whose calm skill impresses me. I reach her classroom of twenty-eight second graders just after morning work time, when the children assemble to share their accomplishments. Everyone is seated on the rug except for Devon, who appears to be looking for something in the writing area. Stephanie's requests for him to join the group are pointedly ignored. Without raising her voice, she finally says, "I'll count to three and then I want you with everyone else." I worry that this strategy will backfire and lead to a direct confrontation. I remember many such failures from my own teaching career, such as the time I discovered Ezra and Kenny hiding behind the large hollow building blocks in the school lobby. Resistant to authority, they adamantly refused to come out just as a tour group of prospective parents led by the director of admissions stopped to talk about the benefits of progressive education. Or the time in the crowded cubby room, where children were putting on their outdoor clothing, when I was so enraged by Michael's ceaseless teasing of others that I held him tightly and shook him far too vigorously. Scared by my rage, he immediately threatened to tell his mother. It was only Roger, the streetwise six-year-old, who could deflate Michael's threat and bring me to my senses when he observed, "That man don't listen to nobody's mamma."

So when Devon fails to join the group after the count of three, I am relieved to see that Stephanie can simply walk over to the writing area, take him by the hand, and bring him to the rug. Throughout this encounter the rest of the children wait quietly and without undo concern for Devon's difficulties. They do not take advantage of the moment to cause other problems and Stephanie herself never loses control of the situation.

After my visits to Stephanie and Catherine's classrooms, I stop to chat with them. The broad range of emotions they display surprises me. Stephanie laughs long and hard over the pseudoadolescent essay that one of the eight-year-old girls has written about the history of friendships in her peer group. Catherine is in a fury about the latest administrative directive that will prevent her from taking informal class trips. Although they are very different teachers, Stephanie and Catherine share a deep appreciation of their young students' difficult lives at the same time as they do not get drawn into emotional entanglements with them. Their lessons about clear boundaries, which ultimately help their students to become effective learners, are what I will take with me at the end of the day. These boundaries, often hard to enforce, enable the children to feel safe in the classroom. I know that I will need to be as steadfast if my parents are to trust me when their own emotions run amok.

When I enter Diane's classroom just after lunch, she is reading aloud to her twenty-two first graders from a book about Michael Jordan, part of a celebration of Black History Month. As I scan the room for a seat, I cannot help but notice the physical disorder. Books are strewn around the carpeted library area, plastic foods have been dumped on the floor in the dress-up corner, and a game of lotto sits partially open on a table. Not finding an extra chair, I lean against the radiator at the back of the room. Within a few minutes I see the reason for the housekeeping difficulties. While most of the class is listening to Diane, Jamal, a short, compact boy, is wandering from area to area, pulling educational materials off the shelves and leaving them where they fall. Diane pointedly ignores this disturbing behavior. When Jamal draws near to me and begins to flip through a stack of photographs from a recent class trip, I naively take this as an invitation to social contact. But my conversational overture is immediately rejected. Leaving the photographs scattered atop the adjacent radiator, Jamal races across the room, opens the door to the hallway, and yells at some passing children. Now sitting on the doorjamb, half in and half out of the classroom, he physically declares his marginal status.

Fifteen minutes into my observation, Diane has finished reading the story of Michael Jordan and is desperately trying to launch a math lesson that requires the class to work in small groups. Several of the children have begun to fight with each other and to openly resist her instruction. Meanwhile, she has pulled Jamal from the doorway back into the classroom. Finally, as he continues to circle around the room, Diane uses the loudspeaker connecting the classroom with the office to request that "security" come to get him. The secretary replies that no one is available to help her at the moment and that Mrs. Williamson, the social worker, is also at lunch. Jamal, hearing this conversation, along with the rest of the class, starts yelling, "I don't want security. I don't want security. I won't go." Faced with this threat and fearful of being sent home, Jamal eventually takes a seat at one of the tables and begins to play distractedly with the math materials.

Jamal's behavior, the active resistance of the other children, and Diane's inability to control the class make me want to flee. I am overwhelmed by the evident distress of this sixty-something woman who is being scapegoated by a group of angry six-year-olds. We stand off to the side and I see the tears in her eyes. Although it goes against my better judgment to become involved in an extended conversation before the children, I cannot help but listen. Diane tells me that along with Jamal there are three others in her class whose doctors have prescribed Ritalin to calm their behavior. Because of difficulties in filing the Medicaid claims, only one of the four is actually receiving his medication regularly. Diane is in an impossible situation and woefully unprepared to manage it. She begs me for suggestions. An intruder in the room, I feel it presumptuous to offer advice. At the same time, remaining silent feels equally inauthentic, an act of supreme bad faith.

Diane's story and Jamal's life are narratives born out of social injustice. They speak to a history in which material resources and cultural capital are inequitably distributed, most frequently along racial lines. Oddly, however, the emotions that Diane and Jamal elicit in me resonate with experiences from a very different world. It seems improbable to write on the same page about Jamal, an African American boy of six growing up in poverty, and my father, a white, Jewish man of eighty-seven living on the Upper East Side of Manhattan. Even as I read that Jamal's neighborhood was once the seat of a thriving Jewish community, I know that my parents are themselves several generations removed from the immigrant experience, let alone the experience of black families who have emigrated from the American south. Even as I know that racism and anti-Semitism may stem from similar roots, and that both have lethal consequences for their victims, I know that the histories of Jews and African Americans are very different.

It is impossible to equate the lives of families living in deep poverty with the lives of my parents. Yet it does seem possible that the demands Jamal places on Diane and those my father places on me give rise to similar feelings of frustration, anger, and helplessness. It is not happenstance that Jamal and my father share some of the same medications. Jamal races about the classroom pulling supplies from the shelves, poking at children, and ignoring his teacher. At times my father sends a sea of faxes, accuses me of stealing his money, threatens lawsuits, and exhausts everyone with whom he comes in contact. Like Jamal, when my father's dementia is active, nothing enters his brain. Rational arguments carry no weight. It is impossible to get through to him. At these times, however, unlike Jamal, my father does not seem to fear the authority of the security guard or the wrath of an angry parent. This has unfortunate consequences for me, since I have undoubtedly assumed the role of security guard in his life, keeping both external and internal threats at bay. It is I who do battle with the psychiatrist when he fails to understand the depths of my father's dementia and its toll on those responsible for his care. It is more desperation than courage that leads me to fight for what both he and I ultimately need—a modicum of control over his overarching anxiety. I too am the court of last resort with the terrible power to remove him from the familiar world and place him in an institution.

Jamal, on the other hand, does not appear to have strong and effective advocates to secure the Ritalin that he needs, nor is anyone available to help him regain control at school. Growing up in a world in which politicians are pushing for more and more testing and standardized, skill-driven curricula, Jamal's present life is being sacrificed for a future that may or may not come to pass. Perhaps I am unduly sensitive to the problem of time, but I worry that concerns about employment in the years ahead distract immediate attention from the Medicaid system that fails to fill Jamal's prescription and the social world that makes such a prescription necessary. I want the same thing for the children in Jamal's neighborhood as I want for my parents in Manhattan, a present that contains the richness of their history and the sense of a meaningful future. Caring for my parents, I see what it is like to be locked in the moment, devoid of all connections backward or forward. They can only think from day to day, their calendar marked by visits to various doctors and visits from other healthcare personnel—therapists, nurses, and caseworkers. Given the narrowing of their physical powers and the heightening of their medical vulnerability, they no longer act as if they can shape the future. They don't look forward. Events that once might have been a source of pleasure, plans for a Thanksgiving dinner or the purchase of an apartment by my niece, are assessed only for the potential risks they hold. The future is filled with anxiety rather than with potential moments to define the self and to leave one's mark on the world.

What has surprised me most is that my parents' inability to look forward is balanced by an equally daunting resistance to looking back.

I remind my father, the former high school football player and college basketball star, of the benefits of regular exercise and encourage him to go outside more often. As I deliver my lecture I recall the way he would deliver the same lecture to me when I first went away to school. Then, he counseled me to take up a sport and to attend Saturday afternoon football games as a way to lift my spirits and participate in the larger social world. Now, I exercise regularly, moving over the years from distance running and tennis, far too hard on middle-aged knees, to swimming and biking. I try to humor my father by reminding him of the wisdom of his own advice and the irony that it is I who has become the sports enthusiast. He refuses to accompany me on my trip back to a time when I could see no future and felt constantly betrayed by my own body and its desires for other men. I think that he should gain satisfaction from knowing that I have learned a lesson from him, but he doesn't. I think that I should understand how so many illnesses have lead to a total self-absorption that excludes reminiscences, but I don't.

Both the past and the future are territories that my father no longer travels to. He judges me, and other caregivers, by what we can do for him today, not by what we may have meant to him yesterday or the promise that we embody for tomorrow. It's no longer possible to appeal to a shared history, to trust that has been built over time. Betrayal is as recent as the last telephone conversation, a refusal of consent to an ill-conceived financial scheme or to call the doctor about a minor discomfort. As my father's body crumbles, so does the architecture of time that once supported it.

At night the scene in Diane's classroom haunts me. I dream that I am a student teacher who has been asked to settle the children before a group meeting. I am unable to get their attention. They ignore me just as they ignored Diane. I wonder at the continuing impact of my days in hard-pressed urban schools. After all, I have seen it before—children out of control, some needing therapy or psychotropic drugs, some needing only a more meaningful curriculum; teachers in tears, unable to maintain order, let alone live up to their ideals. But in the past my parents did not follow me into the classroom with quite the same persistence.

As a young teacher, I learned to recognize the subtle ways in which my personal history influenced my work with children. I tried hard not to project onto them my own childish needs or to demand from them satisfactions more appropriately found in my adult life. Now that the claims of my parents have become so great and my self-doubts about how to manage them so large, my emotions have become more tangled again. The dreams of unruly children and my inability to control them tell the story of my unruly parents and my failed attempts to bring order to their lives.

Diane and I live in different worlds and have very different relationships to our charges. Like Diane, however, I must find a way to contain the anxiety that makes my father unmanageable and worry about the impact of his behavior on those around him. I know what it is to be paralyzed, afraid of someone who is both more vulnerable and more out of control than I am. I beg the experts and rail against the doctors who withhold the more powerful drugs needed to subdue my father's fears. I can only begin to imagine Diane's frustration at the social-service bureaucracies that prevent Jamal from receiving his medications.

Our circumstances are not the same, but the underlying themes ruling Diane's work with children and the care of my parents are similar. I want to be close enough to understand them but distanced enough so as not to absorb their anger and despair. I see this kind of commitment in the detached but mindful ways that Catherine and Stephanie respond to their students. I remember that, like them, I too can be tough in the morning, setting limits and accepting the hostile accusations that follow in their wake, and filled with appreciative laughter at night. The early childhood classroom is the first place where I became responsible for others and independent of my parents. Now, as I make my weekly trips between Manhattan and my research site, it is teaching me further lessons about attachment and separation, loss and recuperation, the young and the very old.

3

The Future in Question

> People don't have to stop being children, they just
> have to be able to be adults as well. If we cultivate
> unbearable choices, we create impossible lives.
>
> ADAM PHILLIPS, *On Flirtation*

Early childhood educators pride themselves on knowing about transitions. We are experts at convincing anxious parents to leave the classroom in the morning and at cajoling others to spend a few more minutes with a distressed child in need of their attention. Despite the chaos engendered by young children anxiously stuffing half-eaten lunches into backpacks, grasping library books and PTA notes while trailing extra sweaters behind them, at the end of the afternoon we try for one final moment in which our students review the day's successes and failures. Endings are important to us. In between these events we have managed to get twenty-six rowdy first graders up to the art room and down to the gym, into math lessons and out of reading groups, onto the playground and back to the classroom just in time for music.

As a teacher educator I continue to help people make transitions—from other fields to education, from roles as parents to roles as teachers, from childhoods spent in traditional schools to more progressive settings, and the reverse. All of these changes have in turn been negotiated to help young children make the monumental shift from intimate, domestic worlds to disciplined, public spaces.

Despite my skills at assisting others, I am always unprepared for my own transition back to school each fall. In mid-August, as the days become cooler and shorter, I inevitably find myself scrambling to revive the writing projects, course outlines, and research proposals that have wilted in the heat of the summer sun. There still seems to be time even as I begin to relive that mixture of excitement and anxiety which as a child I anticipated the new school year with. And no matter what the outcome of my efforts, I always feel unready when September finally arrives.

In the late summer of 1998 the practical and emotional preparations for my return to work were interrupted by my mother's increasingly anxious reports about my father's extreme weakness and recurring moments of disorientation. Monitoring my parents care from a distance and taking into account their multiple health problems, I have tried not to act precipitously and to listen carefully for signs of critical changes. I fear that my own life may all too easily be subsumed by their many needs. I guard my energies as well so as not to squander them on false crises and to exhaust myself before the more serious, terminal events have begun.

On Sunday my mother asks when I will come to the city. Reminding her that I will be there on Tuesday, she says, "Good, because I need you." For someone not given to direct demands on others, her words are startling. They signal that indeed something is seriously wrong.

On Monday morning, however, I conveniently "forget" the urgency of my mother's words until the health aide who tends my father calls. Calm and competent, Marlene summarizes the situation, saying, "He can't go on this way." Ten minutes later, when I tell my father that I have arranged a doctor's appointment for later that morning, he tells me that he won't go. He works hard to prove that he is not disoriented, knows the day of the week, and can recite details of a favorite nephew's weekend visit and the list of medical specialists whom he is to see in the coming days; he insists that he has no time for another appointment.

My father and I are now plunged into a familiar game in which I am the judge of record, assessing the truth of his situation in a court of last resort. My father is determined, uncanny, and persuasive as he pleads his case by demonstrating his physical and psychological competency. The very skills that my father summons to his defense indicate the depth of his fear and desperation. They also indicate the continually shifting nature of power in our relationship. Although I have legal authority to make difficult decisions, he has the ability to inflict the anguish and pain of a helpless father pleading with his son. Power is never unidirectional, but circulates between us. As our conversation ends, I ask my father to reconsider at the same moment as I make mental preparations to leave for New York.

Two hours later the call from the doctor tells me that my father has consented to be seen and is suffering from an infection and severe dehydration that require immediate hospitalization. My father accepts the antibiotics, ten dollars per pill (my parents' antiquated health insurance does not include any drug coverage), promises to drink plenty of liquids, a physical impossibility due to prior throat radiation and surgery, and returns home. Steadfastly refusing the hospital, my father poses a direct challenge to medical authority and to me. I face moments like this with equanimity and with dread, confused by our changed relationship. He is the headstrong father I have always known, determined to assert his will at every turn, as well as the extremely vulnerable octogenarian who longs to be taken care of. I am the adult responsible for his care and the child who continues to want his approval.

I have not always been willing to recognize these multiple, sometimes contradictory roles. For the longest time I simply wanted to believe it was over—childhood, that is. I stubbornly persisted in this belief, ignoring all indications to the contrary, until the day shortly before my mother's first illness in 1996 when I was called to sort through the boxes containing the long-forgotten remnants of the past.

In a hurry, I was annoyed with my parents as I began to open the cartons and empty the dusty closet shelves. The memories started slowly but soon picked up momentum, becoming an unstoppable tide. Here was the heavy metal erector set stored in its own red box, replete with pictures of bridges, machines, and vehicles that my brother and I tried to duplicate without success during those long, house-bound days of winter. There was the stamp collection carefully packed away along with our hopes of finding rare misprints that would make us rich, the glassine envelopes still filled with garish triangular stamps depicting exotic flowers and majestic animals from faraway places— Tanganyika, Costa Rica, the Republic of Cameroon. And the old cigar boxes, lined with cotton batting, containing the hand-painted lead soldiers purchased by a beloved aunt and uncle on their first trip abroad after the War, essential props in elaborately staged conflicts of our own devising.

A single afternoon was all that was needed to decide what would be saved for my niece and what would be consigned to the display cases of the local thrift shop. That was the easy part. It was much harder to sort through the emotions that the objects elicited. I was drawn to savoring the pleasures of recollection at the same time as I was fearful of sinking into the swamp of nostalgia. Childhood memories can bring to the fore ambivalent emotions and unresolved relationships that threaten the achievement of adulthood. Middle-aged, I wanted to fix my understandings of the past so as to better focus on the future, to see myself as making history rather than determined by it.

Recent events had broken through the pretense that childhood belongs only to the past, another country which we may visit or ignore at will. For as my parents and I struggled to meet the demands of illness and aging, the complexity and vitality of our relationship became clear. Regardless of age, we continued to be parent and child. We brought our shared history and ways of relating to every interaction. At the same time, I saw new qualities in their personalities—my mother's anxiety and depression, my father's determination, dare I say ambition, to make the most of his life. Were these new character traits, the result of their changed situation? Or were they part of my growing up that I just hadn't seen?

With time, however, memories fade, facts are confused, history intervenes. Because memory is never pure but always colored by successive layers of experience, it does not offer a direct route to the past. I found it difficult to sort out what I actually remembered, what had been described by my parents, and what I was learning about my family through looking at old photographs, report cards, and first attempts at writing that had been carefully packed away in boxes and stored deep in the back of closet shelves. I realized that what is important to me is not the literal accuracy of the stories but the emotional truths that they are the vehicles for. I saw that it is these truths that both connect me to the past and that I would need to reconfigure in order to do what was necessary in the present.

I began to doubt my once-secure memories of parents, childhood, and the larger narrative into which I wove them. That narrative, which remained unedited from my midtwenties to midfifties, was now open to, indeed demanded, reinterpretation. I realized that the life narratives we construct are more about coming to terms with the present than any truth about our history. Perhaps childhood itself is not a fixed part of the past that can be known with any certainty. At first blush, the idea that childhood is constituted by an elusive, fragmented collection of memories and that our lived experiences are open to multiple interpretations challenges the commonsense understanding of our early years as a foundational period when the building blocks of later successes and failures are put into place. Yet my recent experience suggested the fragility of memory and an ever-evolving understanding of what it means to be young, and to have lived in this particular family at that time in history.

Despite recent research on the abilities of children to overcome early learning difficulties, on childhood resiliency in the face of social adversity, on the potential of lifelong learning, and even on the continuous regeneration of brain cells, educators and parents are often reluctant to give up their belief in the critical importance of the first years. Anyone who doubts this need only review the guidelines for Developmentally Appropriate Practice published by the National Association for the Education of Young Children, with its specific, detailed recommendations for how to run the best possible program for young children. The aisles of the local bookstore, stacked high with self-help manuals telling parents how to foster their children's confidence and competence, convey the same message: do it right in early life or risk the consequences for later development.

The popular media are quick to reinforce this message about the critical role of the early years when they erroneously imply that the results of neuroscientific research on early brain stimulation can be directly translated into the design of educational environments. More toys and activities, more specialists and highly fragmented days, do not necessarily make for smarter, happier, or more engaged learners. It's just not that simple.

The demand for simplicity, however, goes to the heart of the problem. Adults want to believe that they inhabit a logical cause-and-effect world. After all, it's easier to live with certainty and determinism than with contingency and possibility. We are reluctant to acknowledge that our connections to the past and to the children before us are messy, multidimensional, and continuously shifting.

In 1968, when I entered the early childhood classroom, I vividly recall telling people who questioned my career choice that educators can have a critical impact on children when they are very young. My best friend had taught with great enthusiasm in the initial summer of Head Start, and like him, I understood social change as a grassroots process and those roots as best nurtured in the early years.

Today, my graduate students continue to believe in the foundational nature of the early years that will set the pattern for later development. They tell me that they want to teach because they have always loved children and have never had a vocational doubt. Or, like myself at their age, they want to change the world through education, often a more recently acquired desire. Perhaps because of the need to create a distance between past and present, and to experience themselves as responsible adults, capable of being caregivers, they emphasize the differences between children and adults. Despite the subtleties of some developmental theory and the messiness of their lived experience, students portray the road from childhood to adulthood as orderly and well marked. They have read the seminal thinkers—Erikson, Freud, Piaget—and come away with a simplified template.

While each of these theorists writes about different if overlapping domains of development—emotional, cognitive, psychosocial—they all document universal stages of development through which everyone passes, albeit at varying speeds. Change is linear, sequential, and progressive. On the way to graduate school, for example, many of my students have come to believe that the basic struggle between parent and child over attachment and separation is concluded by age three. Caring for my parents, however, I am realizing something quite to the contrary. After all, we are still striving to understand how we are alike and how we are different. We grapple with the changing responsibilities and gifts that result from our close connection. And most importantly, I continue to learn and to know through the body, not just through words. A renewed intimacy occurs as I help my father to navigate from bed to bathroom, shamelessly discuss the daily difficulties of a bladder and bowel gone awry, or simply run my hand across the brittleness of his malnourished shoulders.

Most developmentalists would have us believe that adulthood is a time of new and therefore better powers. Theirs is a story of progress and enlightenment. But perhaps adulthood is a time in which we have expanded but not necessarily improved our tools for making sense of our experience, and when we all benefit by staying in touch with childhood ways of being in the world. It is the context that elicits and shapes our current responses, and in the context of parental care, I am almost always both child and adult.

• • •

When I arrive at my parents' house late that August night, my father is still refusing to go to the hospital. He is waiting up for me along with my mother, the aide, Marlene, and Anne, my twenty-three-year-old niece. He is seated in a wheelchair, barely able to hold his head up, eyes closing midsentence as his words trail off. Called to attention, he asks for yet another glass of cold water, and has sufficient strength to complain that it is neither cold enough nor full enough. In truth, he is unable to swallow at all; the smallest sip of water precipitates a coughing crisis in which everything is returned.

My father claims to follow me as I lay out the two possible scenarios—voluntary and immediate hospitalization or imminent collapse that will force us to take him to the emergency room against his will. At this moment I cannot imagine leaving him to die at home, nor do I think he is in a condition to make such a decision.

As he nods off yet again, I remember prior conversations, not so far distant in time, that contrast dramatically with our present failed attempt at communication.

We were standing at the bathroom sink in the spring of 1997 as my father indulged in an hour-long bedtime ritual. I was leaving for an extended speaking tour in Australia in a few weeks and worried that he might have a potentially life-threatening fall by getting out of bed unassisted in the middle of the night. Neither my concerns nor his reluctance to accept help were new. But now I summoned a fresh determination to get to the heart of the matter before my trip. I asked if the debilitation caused by so many illnesses had made him want to end his life. I told him that, if he had had enough suffering, we would find a way for him to die quickly and peacefully. I didn't know where these cool, confident words were coming from. Despite having seen recent newspaper articles, TV documentaries, and films on the subject, I had no idea how such a carefully planned death would be accomplished. But I needn't have worried. His slow and thoughtful reply reassured me that "No, it's not *that* bad yet." Reluctantly submitting to my logic, he agreed to call for help in the future.

Now I long for the brevity and directness of this earlier conversation and feel the frustration of my protracted attempts to gain and hold my father's attention. Neither of us is able to say the right thing. I decide to put off further efforts till the morning.

Anne, who has waited in the living room with my mother during this private bedroom interview, wants to know what will happen if my father won't go to the hospital in the morning. Hers is a youthful question that assumes an inevitable drama of opposing wills that can only be resolved by a unilateral decision or the use of force. I feel boxed in by the "what if" nature of her question, which poses life as a matter of stark blacks and whites rather than muted grays and partial compromises. I have no answer for her. She asks questions that I am unready for. I am only prepared to stay rooted in the present.

Despite Anne's prodding questions that push me forward in time, her presence is welcome in an unexpected way. As I slip and slide between my roles as loving child and responsible adult, she reminds me that sometimes my years of accumulated experience can make a difference. Caring for people with HIV/AIDS has helped me to curb my natural impatience and to tolerate uncertainty and indecision. In moments of crisis, I try to stay in the present and to move cautiously; deferral holds open possibilities that we cannot yet calculate. Anxious talk of tomorrow draws us away from the pain of today. It functions as a distraction from suffering we cannot alleviate, wrongs we cannot right.

In the morning when I return to my father's side, there appears to be very little change in his condition. He tries to force food and water down his throat without success, and I continue to try to reason with him. We are both getting nowhere. Then suddenly my mother, who has been silently watching and senses our stalemate, gets up from her chair, walks slowly and painfully across the room, bends over my father and, looking straight into his face, implores, "I want you to go to the hospital. Do it for me. Do it now." I am exasperated and embarrassed by this unabashed begging. But after all my carefully worded statements about choices and control, she speaks directly from the heart. I check my irritation, knowing that this moment is as much, if not more, hers than mine. She is learning, in her eighty-seventh year, to make a demand for herself, to cash in on their sixty-year-old marriage ticket to purchase a few more weeks, months, perhaps years of life together. She has earned the right to speak and soon earns his reluctantly proffered words, "All right, I'll go."

I am more sad than relieved to hear his final consent. I feel that together, my mother and I have broken his will. I tell myself that, given his severely weakened condition, my father's refusal to go to the hospital is neither rational nor reflective of his "true" desires. I tell myself that hydration and the gastronomy tube for direct feeding into the stomach do not constitute radical interventions, though they will prolong his life. Yet confidence that we are doing the right thing seems to slip from my grasp because I keep forgetting that my father is not in possession of his faculties and that we are no longer adolescent son and middle-aged parent fighting over a curfew hour. In concert with my mother, I have helped to orchestrate a Pyrrhic victory in a tortuous battle of wills rather than the kind of collaborative healthcare decision I had hoped would be possible.

In the hours to come I am consoled by the way my father becomes calm, relaxed, and patient. Perhaps he is relieved, but I don't ask. While he is lying on a gurney in the emergency room hallway, an orderly offers him a cup of water. For the first time in weeks he speaks the truth, "Thank you, but no. You see, I can't swallow anything." My father gives himself over to the care of others. There is no dissembling in the hospital. Throughout the following week there is never a moment of recrimination, never a note of anger in his voice. He shows more consistent good humor, even his long silenced sense of humor, than he has in the preceding two years.

Later that first night, reviewing the events of the day, my niece accuses my mother and me of having forced my father into the hospital against his will. I am stung by her words, primarily because they resonate with my own doubts. I have tried to imagine myself in his body at this time. I am not terribly successful, but the exercise tells me that there is much that I don't know, enough so that I don't feel comfortable making an end-of-life decision for him.

Anne can't understand why my father goes on, given the extreme limitations of his life, but, when pressed, she is reluctant to imagine an alternative scenario to the one that has taken place: my father collapsing in our unprepared midst. She confides that she and her boyfriend have decided on permanent DNR (do not resuscitate) tattoos so that there will be no mistaking their desires. And therein lies the nub of the problem: what are the desires of my father, eighty-seven, frail and frightened?

Over the preceding days I have tried to listen to his behavior as well as his words in my attempt to assess his intentions. While he was refusing to go to the hospital, he feverishly persisted in attempts to eat, drink, and swallow medications. He even said he would go into the hospital if his cancer surgeon, halfway around the world and unreachable just then, ordered him to go. He did not want to accept responsibility for prolonging his own life. Once in the hospital, he is an active participant in his recovery, taking pride in the total hours he manages to sit in a chair, an important element in recovery from the pneumonia with which he will ultimately be diagnosed, and voluntarily initiates small exercises geared to improve his circulation.

While I once thought my father would not want to suffer unduly or to live with severely diminished capacities, I am learning something different. As life narrows, it becomes that much more precious. My niece has a very different perspective. Despite the periodic career anxieties and personal identity crises that I imagine may cause her to doubt the future, she does have a lifetime ahead of her. Ripping out a few tattered, barely legible pages at the end of the book of life may seem reasonable. Most of the preceding pages have not yet been written anyway, and it is impossible to imagine the subtleties of plot that will knit together the beginning and the end of the text. At fifty-four, having passed life's midpoint, I have begun to experience some of the inevitable failings of the body that may foreshadow the final chapters. I have learned to live with physical limitations that would have been unacceptable a scant ten years ago. Besides, I have known too many people with HIV/AIDS to think that we can predict the future or that death always comes at the end of a full life.

My father wants to live at all costs. He also wants to live on his own terms. When the terms are no longer his to make—if they ever were—he feels caught in a vise of unacceptable choices. He wants the feeding tube, which he sees as a sign of further medicalization and loss of control, only if additional surgery on his throat fails. At the same time, he knows that he will not live to have the surgery unless he agrees to the feeding tube. He wants the tube and doesn't want it. He tells me that these opposing desires are not contradictory, and he is right. Paralyzed by what he sees as untenable choices, he forces me to decide for him. I give primacy to his overriding commitment to go forward and momentarily set aside the feelings of defeat elicited by the compromises that this entails.

In the end, the story of this hospitalization turned out not to be a dramatic one of choosing life or death but a far murkier tale about my father's further loss of physical and mental control. The underlying subtext is my assumption of responsibility for deciphering his desires. There will be no philosophically considered, carefully modulated, Kevorkian death for my father. He will want all the interventions and fight at every turn to have his way.

I am honored by my father's trust and the intimacy that has grown between us. At the same time, I am angered by the new burdens he has placed on me and unnerved by his refusal to make critical decisions for himself. Perhaps my head is filled with too many film and television images of people in midlife who, when faced with a terminal illness, choose to die peacefully surrounded by family and friends. Or reports from my own friends about elderly parents who, when faced with certain suffering and death, stopped eating and drinking. Clearly some people in their final weeks or months are able to sort through their options, identify the quality-of-life limits they might tolerate, and orchestrate an ending that makes sense to them. My father, in contrast, seems to have turned a corner that makes such calculations impossible. Perhaps, given his constitution, they would never have been possible.

One thing is certain, the time for existential conversations about contingency and possibility, choice and mortality, is long gone. The terms for these deliberations set out by Camus and Sartre, Malraux and Beauvoir—the bad faith manifested in denying possibility, succumbing to fixity, and believing that time will not run out—still ring in my own ears. But they were laid down in another era, by thinkers who were faced with other kinds of life-and-death decisions necessitated by political and social commitments. For his part, my father sees no acceptable choices, there is no future worth living for, and good faith is a luxury that younger men concern themselves with. At the same time, he can hardly be said to be giving up and clearly does not want to die. Propelled forward by anger and anxiety, he pursues the impossible, a life without hope in the future, a life in which minute-to-minute, day-to-day survival is all that really matters.

My own days are now framed by the essential moments of the human condition, our natality, how to conceive of and nurture the beginning of life, and our mortality, how to live alongside someone who is dying. To me, caring for the very young and the very old is best understood as an ethical responsibility, a societal good in itself that should be separated from any ideas about future rewards. In a democracy that celebrates autonomy, self-sufficiency, and the accumulation of capital for the future, it may be especially hard to focus on the moment-to-moment needs of the dependent. The rewards of care are less tangible and the challenges to our value system that much greater.

My niece finds it difficult to look directly at my father's situation and shuts out the confusing emotions that it elicits. In a similar way, when scientists and educators define children as undeveloped, they collude in trying to keep at bay the sometimes threatening emotions that are buried inside us. Locating irrational, impulsive, and pleasure-seeking behaviors in children allows us to see ourselves as rational, in control, and altruistically motivated. I am afraid that too often, well intentioned caregivers such as my parents turn children into a serviceable other, one that reinforces their own identities as adults and justifies their control of young people's lives. Like my parents more than half a century ago, professionals today believe that children require constant watching to insure that they do not get out of hand and challenge adult ways of organizing the world. Assisted by all manner of new technologies, classrooms, afterschool programs, and summer camps are set up to keep children physically in view at all times while increasingly sophisticated psychological assessments and academic tests bring to light qualities once hidden from sight.

And perhaps, for Anne and myself, it is no different with the elderly. We are frightened by what we see. My father forces me to confront mortality, to feel old before my time. I try to keep some distance in word and deed. If I describe him as needy, failing, and deeply depressed, then surely I am self-sufficient, thriving, and optimistic. If I declare him irrational and out of control, then surely I am reasonable and in charge. How can I possibly know what it would be like to live with all my senses askew and basic biologic functions mediated by mechanical devices or the assistance of others? How can I know what it means to have little regard for past accomplishments and future projects? Like children, the elderly force us to reorder our priorities, to step back from our concerns for tomorrow, and attend more closely to this day.

I was in graduate school when I first began to develop my criticisms of child development theory. Skeptical of the way it functions to distance teachers from their students, I wanted to explore the common ground adults share with children, the existential themes and ways of knowing that bind us together in one world. Other early childhood specialists were curious when I asked them to consider what is gained and what is lost when adults define children as "undeveloped," in need of just the right amount and kind of protective nurture to mature properly. Ultimately, however, my peers in the field were unable to give up the security of the child development canon. When I completed my doctoral work, I was often a finalist, but did not receive the job offer I sought—a tenure-track professorship.

Then my words were couched in philosophical and political language. Now there is a much larger body of empirical evidence to substantiate my criticisms of developmentalism and educational practices that continually direct us toward the child's future. Now too I have a heightened sensitivity to time gone by and of the options no longer available to my parents or to me. At first, I did not realize how threatened I felt by their despair, their lack of hope. But over time, I have come to understand the central place of hope in our arsenal of survival strategies. In hope we defend against the past; the future will be better. In hope we implicitly acknowledge our disappointments; something wasn't right back then. Hope allows us to imagine a state of affairs in which the past is ameliorated and our deepest losses are compensated.

Theories and practices focusing exclusively on what children will become rather than what they are, however, reflect a kind of blind hope. Blind, that is, because it defends against remembering the ravages of personal and social histories. I think of myself as an advocate for a more modulated form of hope built on a willingness to look at the present and back at the past without allowing ourselves to be overcome by what we see.

Adults are hopeful because of the children. Children in turn contain this precious investment made by their elders. When time and illness destroyed my parents' defenses and left them quite naked, they took little interest in my potential or my accomplishments. It was not my desire for their approval, although there is always that, but the withdrawal of their investment that signaled our changed relationship and triggered my deepest anxieties. Despite their many weaknesses, my parents were still powerful in ways that I am sure they didn't imagine. I was angry about their ability to deprive me of the status they conferred at my birth, emblem of hope. At the same time I accepted their new self-absorption; after all, they were finally leaving the future to me.

4
Psychic Reality

> [A] life as led is inseparable from a life as told—
> or more bluntly, a life is not "how it was" but how
> it is interpreted and reinterpreted, told and retold:
> Freud's *psychic reality*.... So perhaps a metaphysical
> change is required to alter the narratives that we
> have settled upon as "being" our lives.
> JEROME BRUNER, "Life as Narrative"

Growing up, each of us builds an understanding of who our parents are and how our family functions. We construct an overarching narrative of our life and tell particular stories that capture the complex interpersonal dynamics that thread their way through our days. We tell these stories over and over again because they enable us to make sense of our experience and lend credence to the larger narrative. We come to believe in their reality. Over time these stories, our memories of the past, become fixed, and reinterpretation less likely.

Although my work is bound up with children and the role of autobiography in teacher education, my own childhood stories remained as immutable as anyone else's. For me, however, when the overarching narrative finally became unsettled, it was not by a "metaphysical" change but by my parents' all too physical decline and the frequent bedside scenes that followed.

The first time my mother lies in the critical care unit of a local hospital, in the spring of 1996, with her long hair unpinned, released from the tight French roll in which it is usually bound, I am stunned to see glimmers of youthful openness in her face. The medical crisis has caught her off guard, and she reveals an emotional accessibility that had disappeared many years ago. It is as if the surgeon's knife has not only cut out the bleeding ulcer but also punctured an invisible wall surrounding her inner self. Here once again is the conscientious young parent capable of genuine empathy and pleasure in the achievements of her child. At the same time as I am thankful for this opportunity to think of my mother as the loving caregiver, I see with greater clarity the person she has become—fearful, anxious, and suspicious of others.

My mother had once projected competence and confidence. A social worker and businesswoman, she had lived through two successful careers. At home, continually challenging my extreme shyness, she encouraged me to be more adventurous—to climb to the top of the jungle gym unaided, attend a second-grade classmate's birthday party, or risk the terrors of sleepaway camp. Whatever fears and insecurities my mother may have had at that time were kept in check by a stronger sense of parental responsibility.

In contrast, my father, while a loving and engaged parent, was subject to severe depression. I did not see him as possessing particular social skills or emotional resilience. In 1997, a year after my mother's hospitalization, just after the first of his surgeries for cancer of the larynx, sitting at his hospital bedside late in the afternoon, I understand something quite different. As he recovers from throat surgery and is still unable to use his newly reconstructed voice box, an unfamiliar nurse is attaching a clear plastic bag of life-sustaining fluids to an IV pole. My father taps the nurse on the shoulder to gain his attention, picks up a yellow pad, and writes a brief note in his cryptic handwriting. The nurse, who has temporarily stopped his work, breaks into a broad smile as he deciphers the words, looks directly at my father, and says "Benjamin," his own name. My father smiles back, and Benjamin returns to the task at hand. I am in awe of this simple interchange. My father is able to generate a life-sustaining fluid of another kind.

As a child, I knew my father to be a demanding, exacting, often exasperating person. Now I also know my father as a person who easily forms relationships. He treats the hospital staff with respect, as individuals. They respond in kind. My father is able to make his way in a large and frightening institution while ensuring some control over the course of his treatment. He skillfully collaborates in his own care when dealing with professionals of one stripe or another.

Although events change people, they also bring out aspects of character that have always existed. The past has become unfastened from its secure moorings in my memory. I wonder if my mother was as confident as she once appeared, as my memory has captured her. Was my seemingly intractable shyness an inherent character trait or the reflection of a complex maternal relationship? I understand that beneath the surface of her always encouraging words, my mother may have communicated deep ambiguity about separation and the risks of independence. Perhaps too my father was far more socially accomplished than I had realized, and my older brother far less able to deal with the "real" world than I had grasped.

Now, when my brother and I are faced with two frail parents, the entire family drama has to be restaged. As a child, I played the role of the "sensitive/creative" younger sibling. Resisting the confines of my middle-class upbringing, I became the black sheep—college dropout, gay man, nursery school teacher. My brother, more competitive and conforming, became a prosperous international businessman.

As adults, we do not live in the same world. It seems as if he has never seen anyone seriously ill; never known anyone who has died. My experience of being a sexual outsider, and of working with young children and people with HIV/AIDS, has given me a different perspective on what matters most in our lives. Within our family I have become the responsible one, grounded in the mundane realities of caring for fragile lives—finding domestic help, speaking with doctors, monitoring finances.

Until the precipitous decline in their early eighties, my parents frequently shared memories of their childhoods and retold our family history. There were the stories of my own childhood—the blizzard of '48 when I was stranded in a snowdrift and the police had to be called; the summer of '50 when I refused to enter the busy dining room of the Catskill resort until everyone sang "Happy Birthday"; the spring of '52 when my father taught me to ride a two-wheeler that had been passed down from a neighboring cousin. I often grew impatient with these familiar renditions of the past as well as with my parents' questions about childhood friends who had long since disappeared from my life. It became hard to tell what I actually remembered and what I had been told, what I had experienced and what my parents wanted to encode as part of the family saga.

Now my parents are no longer so easily seduced by nostalgia. They seldom seek the intimacy that is evoked by the sharing of personal memories. Concerned about my mother's growing withdrawal after her surgery, I proffer invitations to remember herself at other points in time. She does not accept the bait, does not want to recall her full and busy life. Although my father can be both philosophical and practical about the future, surviving the regular medical crises requires all his energy. The unyielding demands of the body imprison my parents in the present.

Ironically, I find myself increasingly drawn to the past. As do most children, when I was growing up I saw my parents as omniscient. My father knew everything from how to count by tens, knot a tie, and hit a home run, to the names of all the state capitals and former presidents of the United States. My mother not only knew small things like how to tie a shoelace or a perfect bow on a birthday present, she also knew deeper psychological truths like the importance of self-confidence and the difficulty of trying new activities. There was always certainty in what my parents did and what they thought.

Entering adolescence, I began to understand that despite their different realms of knowing, they shared a deep belief in the natural superiority of their children. This superiority, when realized through academic distinction and participation in the full panoply of extracurricular activities, would lead to later successes. Acceptance at the right college assures admission to an elite professional school, which in turn lays the groundwork for a life of economic security, perhaps even public recognition. Because the world is a threatening place, we must either enter armed with sufficient credentials to protect ourselves or face the irreversible outcomes of our early mistakes.

I grew up in bondage to the future. And, inevitably, I rebelled —dropping out of college, actualizing my homosexual desires, and rejecting a safe career. I found support for my moment-to-moment orientation among the existentialist writers popular with disaffected youth in the 1950s. They taught me about choice and possibility, resistance and rebellion, contingency and the value of keeping death in front of us at all times. Later, I carried these interests with me into the classroom. As a new teacher, undaunted by Piaget's pronouncements about limited intellectual abilities and warnings from psychoanalysts about potential emotional upsets, I explored the children's here-and-now understandings of death. I decried the absence of books that would help other teachers do the same. Still further on, when AIDS became an overwhelming presence in my personal and professional life, I championed discussions of HIV and other difficult social issues with young children. In this way I continued to resist assumptions about what children can and can't understand, about the differences between the young and the old.

On the rare occasions that my parents become nostalgic about the past, I remind them of their persistent attempts to control my future. My parents acted as if their constant surveillance would assure the outcomes they desired. With this belief, they validated their personal sacrifices and tried to negate the gratuitous nature of life.

My parents were models of self-sacrificing, child-centered caregivers who appeared to have few interests beyond the welfare of their family. Seldom did they display physical or emotional affection toward each other. I sometimes wonder what my childhood would have been like if I had experienced a few healthy doses of benign neglect. What if my overly zealous middle-class parents had spent less time reading about the ages and stages of child development and more time tending to their own needs as adults? As the oldest in his working-class family, my partner, Bob, was privy to some of the pleasurable rituals that his parents indulged in. His mother, who worked as a housekeeper for much of her life, participated in weekly card nights around the kitchen table with her sisters and friends. Highballs were plentiful, off-color jokes abounded, and children were momentarily forgotten. Bob's father, who worked in a factory during the day, played the drums at night. When he was younger there were even engagements at local clubs for his trio.

It's not that my parents lacked for friends, but the tenor of their interactions were different. There were nightly phone calls to my father requesting advice about the stock market, business opportunities, or healthcare decisions. My mother fielded calls and occasional crisis visits from women friends seeking a sympathetic ear about a nasty divorce or an unmanageable depression. For myself, I was fascinated by a bevy of visiting aunts and uncles who would inevitably arrive in New York City with restaurant reservations in place, theatre tickets in hands, and a full calendar of social events planned. Closer to home I was intrigued and intimidated by my mother's sister and her husband who, unlike my own parents, openly displayed their mutual attraction as well as their fierce disagreements, something my parents considered unacceptable. I grew up understanding little about how people live through passionate attachments to each other or the world, let alone how they let off steam and played together.

Revengefully, now as I try to help my parents manage, I want to tell them that all of their conscientious care—their attempts to shield me from discomforting emotions and to provide me with armor against a threatening world—was of no avail. But I don't. All my diplomas didn't protect me from illness or knowledge of death. Nor has my respectable income made me a stranger to personal unhappiness. Above all I want to tell them that I was right about the future and they were wrong. But I don't. I know that to say this would be to say the obvious, to cruelly underline the lessons that their final years are teaching them only too well.

Instead I focus on taking charge of my own memories, and the possibilities of editing them in fresh ways. Perhaps this interest is simply an artifact of time. For, until the recent hospital dramas, I have consciously sought to reassure myself that childhood is securely anchored in the early years, a fixed and knowable entity whose difficult emotions would not intrude upon the present. Through countless hours of therapy as a young adult living on my own, I had gained sufficient distance to cautiously look back at the homeland I had just left and to construct a story that would contain my feelings and explain who I had become. I seldom saw my parents during this period, and, when I did, the meetings were strained and uncomfortable. The psychological journey that I was engaged in seemed to require complete physical separation. I declared a moratorium on direct contact as I struggled to unpack the baggage that I had brought with me from childhood into the adult world.

I emerged from my twenties with a guidebook that helped me to appreciate the people and places of my childhood. Critical images had acquired explanatory captions and freshly drawn maps clarified the routes I had taken to achieve independence from my family. The unruly passions and conflicted relationships of childhood were organized in such a way that they were no longer quite so threatening. This work of putting the past into an understandable set of stories allowed me to move forward with my life, to become a gay man comfortable with a still marginal social identity and capable of intimate, loving relationships.

I have never had a good sense of direction, and throughout my thirties and forties this guidebook allowed me to adhere to familiar ways of interacting and conversational themes when visiting my parents. We always remained on safe, clearly marked highways and steered clear of dangerously ill-lit emotional alleys. These alleys, filled with my resentments over their controlling, intrusive, and ambitious ways, exuded the potential for unbearable emotional toxicity. My parents wanted to hold on to me at all costs and could not imagine a relationship that allowed for greater elasticity and independence. Reliving our early enmeshment did not feel like the way to move into the future but rather a retreat into an unacceptable past.

My feelings were no family secret. Back in my early twenties my mother's sister invited me to afternoon tea. It was an unusual occasion, and once the formalities were completed and we settled in for our chat, I was unprepared for the subject matter—the unfathomable pain I was causing my parents. How could I, the youngest and most beloved of children in our extended family, be so angry and rejecting of my well-meaning parents? What could cause me to place such a distance between them and myself? Despite my deep respect for my aunt —and part of me had to admire this direct intervention on behalf of her sister—I had little to say in response to her queries. It was all still too raw and tender. And what to do about that huge white elephant in the room, my unacknowledged gay life? The determined explorations that had begun in my early teens had resulted in serious if tumultuous relationships with a number of older, married and single, gay men. In those pre-Stonewall days, I could only imagine how news of these relationships would be greeted. Understood? What forms of remediation might my clinically oriented family deem necessary to correct such obvious pathology?

Needless to say, fifteen years later when Bob was introduced into the family circle, his patently loving and steady manner helped to smooth out some of the rougher edges. Of course, as with any child in a committed relationship, it was less easy for my family to infantilize my life or to claim me for their own emotional needs. Nevertheless, when my mother's sister had to make a difficult choice about invitations to an anniversary dinner hosted at an exclusive French restaurant with limited seating, she apologetically told me there was no room for Bob. Outraged, and unwilling to attend, I was persuaded by

Bob that I should not meet her act of estrangement with one of my own. Due to a last-minute cancellation, a place was finally found, but throughout the event memories of prior dinners in this five-star venue underwritten by an early boyfriend served as a reminder of the hidden life that had had its perks.

In retrospect, I see this incident of the early 1980s as occurring midway on the arc of family acceptance. My aunt was embarrassed and apologetic. She knew that she had behaved badly, and such social exclusions did not happen again.

Until my fifties, I have little reason to redraw the maps created in my twenties that had prevented me from getting lost or disoriented when dealing with my parents. Then I discover that the emotional terrain has been slowly transformed by the passage of time and the ravages of disease. I see that new maps are required to guide us through previously unimaginable scenes, such as my father's near death from dehydration and my mother's recurring ministrokes that leave her with many small cognitive impairments.

Indeed, it might be most realistic to say that my father's reluctant hospitalization in 1998 does not end when he is wheeled out the front door into the waiting ambulette. Although he leaves physically stronger than when he entered, he also leaves mentally shaken. With the remnants of a hospital-induced psychosis common among the elderly, he frequently constructs elaborate stories that contain only a grain of truth. Like memories of childhood, his tales of the hospital require that the listener attend to the emotional message rather than literal accuracy of the narrative. The hospitalization itself is bracketed by an inaugural moment when his resistance to admission gives way under the pressure of my mother's desperate plea—"I want you to go. Do it for me. Do it now"—and a concluding moment that takes place two weeks after he is discharged.

Just as on the first occasion, we are assembled in the dining room, my father at the table, my mother on the sofa. Again, my niece has discreetly placed herself in the living room, able to hear but not to participate directly in the conversation. Today my father is opening and sorting his mail, a time-consuming activity that he does with fierce concentration. Hunched over the table, he does not look up when I enter the room, but I can see that his face is drawn and tense. Nor does he offer words of greeting when I place my hands on his brittle, bony shoulders.

I am confused and made uncomfortable by my father's steely silence as I converse with my mother about routine matters. Remembering my visit the preceding week, when my father didn't want to talk about the hospital or his health, I try to navigate the minefield of other potentially explosive subjects in search of safe ground. I receive only the briefest replies to my attempts at conversation. But when I ask about a new system my niece and I have devised for sorting the mail, it is as if I have hit a land mine. He suddenly explodes in a tirade of recriminations about losing control of his affairs and my failure to treat him with respect. His jaw begins to quiver and tears stream down his cheeks. His neck is bent so far over now that his chin is practically touching his chest. I can barely see his face, which seems to have dissolved in a featureless blur. Sobbing uncontrollably, his nose running like a small child's, my father has become unrecognizable.

In retrospect, it could have been any topic that opened the floodgate to my father's emotions. The particular one I chose goes to the heart of his feelings of dependence, his declining ability to care for my mother, and my usurpation of his responsibilities. It's also time to acknowledge the changes brought by the hospital stay, to say that there is no cure and will be no cure for the multiple impacts of age, only a life sustained with ever more supports from others. My father voices regret about the prior medical interventions—the multiple radiation therapies and first throat surgery—that have kept him alive. He wishes he were dead. He continues, he says, for my mother's sake and because he knows she won't live long after him. His words are direct and pitiless.

I am looking at my father and thinking about my mother, wondering if she is able to take in all that he has had to say. By now there are plenty of tears in my own eyes as I try to acknowledge how inexplicably difficult his life must be. At the same time I am impelled to defend our attempts to help him and our commitment to honoring his wishes. I say how painful it is to hear his harsh, unrelenting criticisms of my mother as she tries to minister to his needs with her own limitations and remind him that each of us, in our own way, is suffering the moment. He does not respond to any of my emotion-laden words. Instead, he picks up papers from the table and reads them with intensity born of the desire to quell his own turbulent feelings. For now the bills, receipts, and notices that proliferate at a time in life when we can least manage them protect him from my probing questions and from his own. They connect him to a safer, less threatening world. And I too retreat from the intensity of the moment

It's the summer of 1951. My father has just returned from the hospital after what today would be classified as routine surgery. The French doors leading to my parents' bedroom are closed, an unusual daytime occurrence. As I pass by, I can hear my father crying. I can't see into the room because, like the walls throughout the apartment, the glass panes of the doors are painted battleship gray. Nor would I have wanted to look. I am too frightened and do not understand why my father would be upset about coming home. No one offers an explanation for his sadness. Later, over lunch, my mother suggests that I spend a few days at my grandmother's house while my father recuperates. I feel this to be an honor, a sign of my maturity. Unacknowledged is my sense of relief in this exile from the site of much parental pain.

My grandmother lives only a few blocks away, and I have the run of her apartment. I know every corner but most especially the kitchen with its icebox, upright telephone, and wooden counters. Here she produces cheese and rye bread sandwiches, carefully wrapped in waxed paper and rubber bands, for our daily picnics in Riverside Park. Here too she mixes Coca Cola with milk at meal times to lessen its pernicious impact on my growing body but otherwise indulges all my gustatory whims. My grandmother does her best to entertain me and I am appreciative of her efforts. But by the end of the week I am homesick and feeling my own kind of sadness. At home my father is clearly back in control of his emotions, and I do not hear him cry again.

It is only the following summer that I myself experience the difficulties of a return to once-familiar surroundings. Whereas my father's hospital stay was involuntary, I had eagerly chosen to go away to summer camp. It is the first afternoon back at home, and I am seated in my regular place at the kitchen table with its slightly sticky-to-the-touch oilcloth covering bearing a pattern of clustered, just-ripe cherries. Although it is August, my mother is preparing hot cocoa at the stove, a transitional food to recall the cold mornings I have just spent in the Adirondacks. She is gently quizzing me about the summer. As she knows only too well, I've had a bad time of it. At seven, I was woefully unprepared for the long separation, cried myself to sleep every night, and could barely read her letters or open the carefully wrapped packages without becoming tearful. I forbade either of my parents to call me. The sound of their voices filled me with sadness and longing. Now that I am safely home, looking out of the window past the one tall building that partially obstructs our otherwise dramatic view of the Hudson River and the New Jersey palisades, my emotions are a complete jumble. And much to everyone's surprise when my mother places the hot cocoa in front of me, I burst into uncontrollable sobs. I don't want hot cocoa after all, nor do I want the cold soda offered in its place. Oddly enough, I don't want to be home nor do I want to be back at camp. For the first time in my life, I have become a displaced person.

In retrospect, I understand my tears as tears of ambivalence. They express anger at my parents for having succumbed to my premature demand for sleepaway camp as well as my happiness at being home again. Although I have returned, my trust in their decision-making powers has been shaken. Something has been inexplicably lost at camp that summer, a bond irreparably damaged.

• • •

These memories of childhood separations, of my father's sadness and my own, call me away from the current crisis. They allow me to place some distance between the immediate moment and myself. At the same time, they allow me to place my father's tears in context and to know that they will be managed. Although the 1997 throat surgery saved his life, it left him with a greatly diminished capacity to swallow. The unanticipated insertion of a feeding tube to insure sufficient liquids and sustenance that he has just undergone is a permanent acknowledgment of defeat. My father will not recover the ability to eat or drink as we had all hoped. He has, indeed, experienced a terrible loss. In the hospital he focused on recovery, on coping with the minute-to-minute exigencies of institutional life—the two hours on a gurney in the hall awaiting an x-ray, the stream of unknown doctors and nurses who all insist on asking the same questions about the day of the week and the president of the United States, the new medications and intravenous fluids that must be monitored for fear of error. At home, and with time, my father lets down his guard and experiences emotions that he previously kept at bay, including his deep ambivalence about living with such diminished capacities.

My father, who sits directly across the table, still does not look at me. His head is collapsed into his chest as he continues to randomly shuffle papers. I am aware, however, that our conversation isn't over. Suddenly I find myself asking about the death of my grandfather, and I don't know why. Perhaps I am really asking my father to have sympathy for me, to remember himself as a loving son, and to imagine that I too might have feelings of sadness and rage. Perhaps I want to distract him as well, to help him find comfort in the memory of someone whom he revered and idolized. He tells me that his father died quickly, six months after cancer was diagnosed at the age of seventy-three. At that time my father was only forty-five, nine years younger than I am now. He starts to sob again.

When he first began to cry I wanted to reach across the table and take his hand, but I was afraid he would strike out at me with his terrible anger. Now, newly determined not to be intimidated, I place my hand on top of his tightly clenched fist. It is unyielding to my touch. I am sorry that he rejects a human connection that might offer some comfort. More selfishly, I feel helpless in the face of his despair and disappointed that he does not recognize my own efforts on his behalf, but he has nothing left to give anyone else.

Finally, my mother, who has been silently watching this scene, gets up from the sofa with great difficulty and walks over to my father just as she had done six weeks before. Now she does not plead or seek to persuade. Instead, she simply stands behind him and puts her arms around his shoulders. She runs her hands along the back of his neck and across his chest without saying anything. I fear that he will push her away too. Miraculously, he accepts her reconciling touch, slowly stops crying, and begins to collect himself. He looks exhausted but calmer. I am taken aback by this receptiveness to her ministrations and pleased that something other than his bitterness and recriminations can still pass between them.

The next day my mother begins our phone conversation by uncharacteristically crowing, "I bet you were surprised, didn't think he had it in him." She expresses pride in my father's honest display of emotions but will take no credit for her ability to comfort him. As I continue to remark on her quiet but starring role in the drama, she says modestly, "Well, there's a lot of history there. It ought to be worth something." And yet, from my perspective, it is that very history that makes my mother's ability to offer succor, not my father's display of emotion, the most remarkable part of the story.

Despite its modern trappings, my parents had a traditional marriage. First cousins who grew up in different cities, they only came to know each other as young adults. A certain kind of snobbery made marriages among close relatives in Jewish families (my grandmothers were sisters) not uncommon in those days. Who else would be good enough? While both my parents attended Ivy League colleges before dating each other, it was my mother who earned an advanced degree. A photograph taken circa 1936 for my mother's official identification card as a "New York City Social Service Provider," shows a slender, delicate woman of twenty-six whose long hair is pulled back softly and knotted at the nape of the neck. She wears a plain blouse, wool skirt, and suede jacket left open. The appearance is neat yet informal, serious yet relaxed. It is easy to imagine her as the good student she was, someone who studied the new, Freud and Franz Boaz, as well the old, German and Yiddish. It is also easy to imagine her as the kindly and sympathetic listener who pursued a career in social work until the birth of my brother in 1941. My mother maintained her membership in the official social work association until the end of her life. She often explained with great pride that, despite her father's distant and traditionally patriarchal demeanor, he insisted that both his daughters attend college, by no means a given in the early 1930s, and even graduate school to prepare for independent careers.

Dedicated to raising her children, my mother returned to work outside the home only when I was eleven and my father's business was in difficulty. This was the 1950s and I believe that my father, like many men of his generation, felt his wife's second career in commerce rather than social work as a blow to his self-esteem. In deference to his pride, my mother never admitted to liking her work. Of course, since she was also expected to keep the domestic world running smoothly despite the demands of a job that often brought her home well after my father, she may simply have resented holding two positions at once. For myself, I was both proud that my mother worked and angry when the work made her unavailable to fulfill traditional maternal functions.

From an early age, I was keenly attuned to gender-based role expectations. Growing up a sissy, I had endured many spoken and unspoken accusations about possessing the physical and social characteristics of the opposite sex. My feelings told me, however, that I was physically and emotionally attracted to other boys, not that I wanted to be a girl. I was certain of this despite the fact that I was clearly more interested in the satisfactions of the domestic world than the rewards of competitive sports and other stereotypically male activities. At home I enjoyed nothing better than purchasing and preparing the special foods required for holiday meals. At school I was the nascent artist, my most enjoyable hours spent painting and drawing, crafting jewelry, and editing the literary magazine.

While being homosexual—in those days the word itself evoked illicit excitement—meant accepting parts of myself that are usually valued only in women, I did not question my gender identity. In retrospect, this seems all the more surprising given that my peers, regardless of their socially progressive parents, reinforced the confusion between gender and sexual orientation. It was not until the second half of the twentieth century that the concept of gender identity, as separate from sexual orientation, first began to take shape.

When I was growing up the primary stereotype—all male homosexuals desire to be women—informed the "scientific" literature which described gay men as undeveloped and incomplete because of their feminine characteristics. Inevitably, science is embedded in culture, its practitioners human beings who sometimes rise above and more often reflect the prevalent ideas of the time. Despite the theoretical twists and turns of psychoanalytic theory, Magnus Hirschfeld's dictum—homosexuals are women trapped in men's bodies and therefore an intermediary sex—was emblematic of more advanced, dare I say humane, thought. Worse still for me, the only visible homosexuals were the extremely effeminate men I encountered during my adolescence while cruising down Third Avenue and across Forty-second Street with its panoply of enticing pornography shops. Notwithstanding the complete absence of role models, I insisted on imagining a "normal life" in which two men were sexually and emotionally bonded forever, a relationship of absolute equality, devoid of the gendered roles I saw among heterosexuals.

During college I developed an interpretation of our family dynamics that remained unchanged for many years and that cut across the stereotype of distant, inexpressive fathers and close, emotionally attuned mothers. This interpretation defined my father as someone who was deeply connected to his feelings. I read the toxic quality of our relationship during my adolescence, the frequent clashes and smaller misunderstandings, as confirmation of the directness with which he made his demands, stated his case, and knew his own desires. Much to my father's chagrin, I also read his "honesty" as support for pursuing my homosexuality and for not conforming to social pressures.

As a young adult, I continued to be drawn to my father because he represented authenticity and clarity. His sadness and anger, his depression and elation, were always easy to see. In contrast, I felt alienated from my mother's more complex and hidden emotional life. She seemed to make no claims for herself, always the facilitator and peacekeeper; she was quick to test for other people's moods without revealing her own. If no direct reading could be ascertained, my mother did not hesitate to rely on secondary sources—phone calls to a teacher, notes to a tutor, or interviews with a psychotherapist. My mother's concerns were always filtered through an intellectual scrim that concealed her own feelings. She was present but absent all at the same moment.

Although I was aware of their personality differences, I experienced my parents as a team. I don't remember them fighting or even disagreeing, a perception that has been confirmed by many cousins who all recall my parents as loving, protective adults. Dedicated and self-sacrificing, they appeared to have few interests outside of family life. They did very little entertaining and never took vacations without us. Their work lives were spent purchasing education and therapy for their children, something that I found increasingly unsettling as I got older and began to think about my own career prospects. How could two obviously intelligent, well-educated people wind up in jobs that offered so little direct satisfaction? Eschewing conflict, their noses to the grindstone, it was hard to imagine my parents as separate individuals with unique desires or to see the fault lines in their tightly knit relationship.

Over the last decade I have been forced to rethink this image of my parents' lives as going against the gendered grain of our society, my father as deeply emotionally attuned and my mother as more distant and intellectual. Perhaps because I was more focused on what I felt they had done to me than on how they may have inadvertently harmed each other, I looked at their interactions solely in terms of roles. I saw them as having separate if mutually interdependent spheres of activity. When my mother returned to work in order to supplement my father's income, I was completely blind to the fact that, like most other women, she was doing double shifts—one in the domestic world and another in the public. Even though they employed a housekeeper, if anything went wrong it was inevitably my mother's fault. I did not grasp the domestic dynamics that might have been equally well described in the more politically charged terms of oppressor and oppressed. I failed to understand the ways in which their relationship replicated traditional distributions of power and emotion in society.

After my mother's first serious illness, there is a shift in this dynamic. Returning from the six-week hospital stay deeply depressed and withdrawn, my mother is now clearly unable to care for their apartment, to do the daily cooking and cleaning that has defined her life since retirement. In addition, my father's severe spinal stenosis has affected his balance and he requires close, moment-to-moment monitoring. Our fiercest battles in those months are waged in the arena of domestic sovereignty since my mother refuses to acknowledge the extent of her own needs. Eventually she concedes that my father's inability to walk unaided warrants more extensive help. For his part, my father begins to bond with the health aides as he recognizes that my mother cannot fulfill his personal needs. Unable to take on her traditional caregiving roles, my mother becomes something of a displaced person. Increasingly, my self-obsessed father treats her dismissively as a secondary character in the drama of his own survival.

And yet, slowly and painfully over a two-year period, my mother's depression lifts. Making a connection with a particularly sympathetic health aide, she is able to find a new role for herself—making doctors' appointments and keeping the all-important weekly calendar, answering the phone, and maintaining contacts with the outside world. As she begins to reposition herself in the domestic sphere, she comes back to life and into touch with her feelings. For the first time in decades, my mother is able to express genuine sadness, to enjoy a bit of humor, and to speak more realistically about her situation. She even learns to make some small claims for herself—telling my father, when I am present, that she does not like to be yelled at for unimportant reasons, that she wants to go out to a restaurant with a visiting relative, and that she will attend a family function that he refuses to go to.

My father continues to act out his patriarchal role with a vengeance. He is constantly critical, and my mother is always trying to please him. Now I understand their interactions as anything but atypical. It is as if all the illness and vulnerability has finally laid bare the gendered skeleton of their relationship. With my father's emotions writ so large, what place can there have been for my mother's desires? With her endless self-denial, how can he learn to curb his demanding ways? Finally, I am left to wonder what I gained and what I lost by not seeing the extent of his bullying and the depths of her self-abnegation. What do these changed perceptions tell me about myself, about the function of memory, and the childhood I thought I understood so well?

A year and a half after my father's hospitalization for severe dehydration and the insertion of the gastronomy tube, much to everyone's surprise, he comes back to life. Slowly I watch as he sheds the flattened and sanitized language with which he left the hospital. Increasingly his talk is punctuated by favorite Yiddish expressions, terms of childhood endearment, and the sounds of genuine laughter. And although both my parents have never lived in the past, as it is reported of some elderly, my father is now more willing to tell anecdotes about his family and to recall the impact on his life of historical events such as the Great Depression. Feeling less vulnerable and more robust, he is able to look back, and this, ironically enough, allows me to stay anchored in the present.

Despite the definitive prognosis of his own doctors, my father continues to seek out the one medical expert who can explain with certainty the nature of his swallowing difficulty, know how to treat it, and assure him that he will eat again. Meanwhile, he sits at the dinner table while my mother and I have our food. He encourages us to eat more—my mother, because she has always been anemic and is now dangerously underweight, and me, because over the years that's just become an immutable part of the family script. He is genuinely pleased to hear that the curried chicken is tasty and disappointed when I reject a second helping of mashed potatoes. We reminisce about the way that my mother used another orangey yellow ingredient, saffron, to flavor special dishes and even agree to disagree on whether he ever enjoyed spicy foods himself.

At times my father complains about the discomfort caused by his feeding tube. It irritates the skin, makes odd noises, and occasionally causes minor bleeding. As in so many other areas of his life, my father adjusts to discomforts that once would have been considered intolerable and sets his sights on increasingly modest accomplishments. He does not speak of missing my mother's famous pot roast or of longing for the taste of her potato pancakes. More simply, he hopes one day to sip a glass of water or to drink a cup of tea without choking. I try to steer a middle course between the Scylla of supporting goals that can only lead to disappointment and the Charybdis of blocking the ambitious drive that has served him so well. Whatever the outcome, we are able to talk and share stories, summon old memories, and even create some new ones. If for no other reason than that, a year after his hospitalization for severe dehydration, both of us are enjoying an improved psychic reality, the best it has been in a long, long time.

5
Reading, Writing, and
the Wrath of My Father

> I want to suggest that anthropologists, and other
> vulnerable observers, can and should write about
> loss. But we must do so with a different awareness,
> an awareness of how excruciating are the paradoxes
> of attachment and displacement. Above all, I think
> we need to be absolutely pitiless with ourselves.
> RUTH BEHAR, *The Vulnerable Observer*

My personal and professional lives have a serendipitous way of running along parallel tracks. Ever since my father was diagnosed with cancer of the larynx, I have had to think about the possibility that he would lose the ability to speak. How would he communicate? What would happen to his love of language? At the same time, as codirector of research for a large urban school-reform project, I am confronted with the overwhelming focus on reading and writing in contemporary classrooms. Observing teachers and students in a hard-pressed, low-performing district, I am painfully aware that a pernicious insistence on measurable standards, high-stakes tests, and accountability has filtered down to even the youngest children and their teachers. In these early childhood classrooms, every activity must contribute directly and visibly to teaching academic skills. The morning message, once written by teacher to students at the start of the day as a vehicle for encouraging discussion of past experiences or upcoming events, is now a formulaic exercise designed to teach letter and word recognition. When children are invited to bring in a favorite stuffed animal, the activity is rationalized with a measuring assignment during work time. The kindergartners must determine the tallest and shortest creatures brought from home. While reading storybooks, teachers emphasize the names of authors and illustrators, ask children to draw inferences from pictures, and direct attention to techniques of character and plot development. Seldom is a text left unanalyzed and rarely are the author's words allowed to wash over the children, the meaning and structure seeping into their pores without articulation. There is little time for cooking and block building, for trips into the neighborhood and visits from people who do interesting work. In these, as in so many classrooms around the country, literacy takes precedence over life.

Although phonics, spelling, and punctuation are drilled daily, in some classrooms the legacy of the whole language movement is evident in the labels affixed to cabinets, shelves, educational materials, even chairs and tables. I can't help but wonder what the five- and six-year-olds make of the signs mandated by the district to appear over classroom work areas, such as "This is the dramatic play area. We are doctors and nurses. We have fun." Or of the mobiles filled with poems that float too far above the children's heads for them to read, or the "word walls" crammed with too many words for a nonreader to sort through. Although children are required to write in journals and to share their efforts with the class, group discussions that reflect the world outside the classroom are few and far between. As long as they write it really doesn't matter what they say. And for all the talk about multiple drafts, editing, and the writing process, there is an underlying emphasis on the product that will be read to the class, placed on the wall, and ultimately brought home to family.

When in 1999 my father's cancer returned and he lost the remaining part of his larynx that had been salvaged in the initial surgery, I was prompted to reflect on the power and limitations of language in an even more immediate way. Too debilitated or simply too stubborn to master the electrolarynx, an appliance that allows many to communicate despite the lack of vocal cords, my father remains wedded to the written word. Steadfastly refusing a simple instruction such as "milk" or "sweater," he turns every request into a paragraph-long treatise on his current health status or the climate conditions in his room. He takes obvious satisfaction in his carefully crafted sentences, which range in mood from playful and humorous to angry and demanding. When he finally hands me the yellow legal pad on which he scrawls his communications, his expression is one of pride and watchfulness. Will I laugh at the right place, grasp his double entendre, or appreciate his concerns? Although I often wish for the more rapid, more "natural" dialogue possible with the electrolarynx, I can't help but be awed by his command of pen and paper. Despite his numerous disabilities, he is still able to generate ideas, exercise control, and make his desires known in his own unique voice. My father teaches me about the compensatory pleasures of the text.

I only have to look back to my parents' inaugural use of the telephone answering machine to find a precursor to the precise, carefully calculated style that my father would adopt in his written communications. It took my then eighty-something parents several years to master the art of leaving a message. Unlike my friends who have honed their telephonic skills on outgoing messages—adding and deleting musical serenades as well as chipper and Zen-like encouragements for the day ahead—my parents focused their attention on the messages they left on others' answering machines. Over time they turned it into a distinct and nuanced vehicle of communication.

At first, there was only the clicking sound of their hanging up that announced the call. Our recorded message always seemed to catch them off guard. Was it simply that they couldn't organize themselves quickly enough to say anything, or that they felt the machine to be a personal affront, a mechanical barrier designed to prevent privileged parent-child communications? Eventually there were brief, cryptic fragments that ultimately gave way to more fully realized, if formulaic, communications.

My mother's are the briefer. First, she calls out my name as if entering a house and trying to determine if anyone is home: "Johnny, are you there?" Hearing no reply, she identifies herself, "It's your mother." Of course this is totally unnecessary, for who else but a mother would use a long-discarded childhood diminutive, Johnny. Finally, she asks that I call "when you have a chance." While outwardly signaling respect for my full schedule, this last phrase implicitly underlines the need to make my return call a top priority.

For his part, my father is more playful and has developed the phone message into a literary genre. There are still moments when he stumbles, pregnant pauses from which I worry he won't recover quickly enough to avoid a broken connection. But then the hesitant, sandpapery voice, the result of the first surgery and subsequent radiation therapy, returns with new assurance. Unlike the uniformity of my mother's messages, my father's vary wildly in length. His style is eclectic, dare I say postmodern. The structure is that of a business letter with opening address and closing salutation. The overall impact, however, is that of the carefully crafted camp letter, the kind I used to receive as a child in the 1950s. No faxes, e-mails, or telephone calls in those days. Growing up in New York City, I was packed off to the Adirondack Mountains for two months each summer—no wimpy, one-week specialty camps. Luckily, my parents were conscientious correspondents. My mother's letters were chatty and upbeat while my father's were more tightly controlled missives. Given his busy life, it was the fact of the letter that had to be appreciated.

Now, forty-five years later, with more time on his hands, he has clearly come to appreciate the communicative potential of the well-left phone message. The address is always direct, an emphatic call to attention, "Jonathan. This is your father speaking." His commanding opening is then followed by a disclaimer made in a gentler, more relaxed tone, "This is not a medical emergency. We are both fine. Well, actually, there is no change in our physical condition." Here my father adjusts his initial assessment of "fine," which implies an acceptance of their many new disabilities, to a "no change" status. He skillfully edits his words to achieve greater literal accuracy and emotional authenticity. He describes but prefers not to pass judgment on their condition.

My father's request, the reason for the call, is couched in formal language appropriate to the world of business in which he spent most of his life. "Please call me at your earliest possible convenience." Now there is one of those long, unnerving pauses followed by a second disclaimer. "Nor is it about fiscal matters," the topic of many tense phone calls during the last years. "There is something that I want to talk with you about," a shorter pause, "and it's not a problem with the help, either," another arena of ongoing difficulties for us. Finally, the closing salutation echoes those long-ago summers, "Love, Pop."

My father signs his missive with the term he uses to refer to his own father, not the way that I refer to him. I have adopted the more formal "dad." With its increased distance, this form of address allows me to talk with greater ease about routine matters related to sustaining the body as well as to managing life-threatening illnesses. My father identifies with his father, Nathan Silin, for whom I was named, who died before I was born. I am more comfortable removing myself from such a generational link in order to fulfill my caregiving responsibilities.

My father's message is teasing and seductive, a side of his personality that only becomes visible to me late in his life. He tells me what the call is *not* about while refusing to reveal the actual reason of the call. At the same time, he heightens the drama by reminding me of all the potential sources of apprehension. He provokes my curiosity and tries to lure me into a speedy response. He is a master strategist, determined to get my attention.

There will be no record of my parents' success at coming to terms with modern telecommunications. My phone machine has a prominent blue delete button but no hard drive on which to transfer their messages. No mere recordings, however, could capture the way their brief dispatches resonate with the past, when pen and paper provided a simpler and more fluid, if less rapid, mode of connection. Nor could they capture the feelings of potential loss and vulnerability that this last stage in my parents' life has elicited in me. At the time, I savored their mastery of a new technology, glad that it hadn't obliterated the familiar style that permeated our interactions. I even wondered if I wouldn't turn on my computer one morning and find an e-mail from *Pop@aol.com*.

Now that my father has no voice at all, the juxtaposition of my days in classrooms with young children and evenings at my parents' apartment makes me all the more attuned to the power of written language. My father would be all but helpless without his yellow pad and pen, which allow him both practical communications as well as moments of playfulness and pleasure. Because of the pressures on measurable performance in schools I see too little fostering of authentic appreciation for the written word. Both experiences send me back to childhood, to wonder about my own early struggles with reading and writing.

I was what euphemistically has been called a "late bloomer," although not as late as my older brother, who did not begin to read until seventh grade. My own emergence as an independent reader occurred somewhere around fourth grade. Prior to that that time, I have memories of hushed, concerned conferences between my mother and my elementary school teachers.

One moment stands out. I am seated at a table pretending to read a new book that my second-grade teacher had enthusiastically given me a few days earlier. It is illustrated with gaudy pastel colors and has the toxic smell of fresh ink. The story involves some popular cartoon characters of the day that I have absolutely no interest in. Not even the active commerce in comics among my brother's friends—and I do eye their collections with envy—has seduced me into reading about imaginary animals or people. My own overactive fantasy life, crowded with figures from the real world, has no space for these intruders created by the pens of Walt Disney and the like. I turn the pages every few minutes hoping to appear gainfully employed.

Lucy Pringle, a tall, thin woman in her twenties, circulates through the room that contains just a handful of students. She is a new, well-meaning teacher, as my mother explains to me on several occasions, trying to secure my fuller cooperation in Lucy's attempts to teach me to read. But good intentions aren't enough to win my confidence or that of the small band of defiant second graders who I hang out with. We never miss an opportunity to take advantage of her inexperience.

Now Lucy leans over me with her prominent nose, receding chin, and black-framed eyeglasses, and asks me to read aloud. I stumble over every word with more than three letters and cannot answer the questions that she poses about the story. This encounter, in which the novice teacher who cannot control the class meets the novice reader unable to decipher the words on the page, is indelibly etched in my mind. It is a painful moment of truth in which my ignorance, as well as an abiding sense of shame, is unmasked. I am far too young to understand that it is also the failure of the school—to meet my needs as a learner—that is revealed.

As an adult I carry this moment with me as I visit classrooms today and imagine myself a "classified" child. Here I see many children who have been tested prior to entering kindergarten and found to have learning difficulties. Early in the year teachers must design an IEP (individual education plan) for them, which is then filed with the vice principal. A list of the classified children is posted at the entrance to the classroom for anyone to read. There are three to seven such children in each of the kindergartens that I regularly visit, and it is expected that the teachers will implement the plans without additional help.

Fortunately, my confrontation with Lucy Pringle took place long ago, in a small school where teachers had the time to bolster the strengths of their students as well as to attend to their weaknesses. Despite my reading deficiencies, there were many other arenas in which I could experience success. I recall the pride we took in the rabbit cage we constructed from an old table and some chicken wire in first grade, the feel of the saw dust compound from which we modeled the contours of our second-grade map of New Amsterdam, and the smell of the paint that I carefully applied to the upper reaches of the cinder block wall just outside our fourth-grade classroom. That mural of the westward expansion remained long after I became a teacher in the very same school.

Miraculously, I acquire a few more reading skills by fifth grade, even though I seldom have the desire to open a book. My continuing lack of interest is now revealed during our Thursday morning trips to the school library. I am always anxious and at loose ends during these sessions. A short, gray-haired woman with a quick temper, bad teeth, and smoker's breath, the librarian is a ten-year-old's idea of the perfect witch. Each week she impatiently questions me about my interests to hasten the selection of a book. But I have no ability to name my interests and therefore assume that I have none. "How can you not have any interests?" she demands incredulously. A person of no interests, an uninteresting person, I am mortified by this inquisition. Never doing well under pressure, I settle on a Hardy Boys mystery, consciously attracted by the cover drawing of the two friends and unconsciously drawn by the promise of scenes depicting illicit intimacy between them. Will they have a sleepover and be forced to share the same bed? Will they unexpectedly end up at the town swimming hole without their bathing suits? When a quick scouting foray into the text yields none of the desired moments, I disappointedly check it out anyway. During the week, I read so slowly and unenthusiastically that I cannot remember the plot, let alone finish the book.

Until I enter high school and begin to receive letter grades, I think I am very stupid, at least when it comes to academic matters. Then writing rather than reading becomes the terrain of interpersonal struggle and the one on which I feel most inadequate. My grammar and syntax are awkward, my paragraphs filled with non sequiturs and my spelling unrecognizable. Nightly responsibility for editing my papers alternates between my mother and my father, the former far more patient and the latter always insistent that I understand the principles underlying his corrections. I am impatient, easily frustrated, and unwilling to internalize the lessons they struggle to teach me. In the end, I am never quite sure who is the real author of these anguished collaborations. They reflect my deep ambivalence about being held accountable for my own words, my own life.

This reluctance to claim my ideas on paper, I now believe, was connected in some complicated and still incomprehensible way to my recalcitrant and unacceptable sexuality. The written word was both the medium that tied me to my parents in endless battles over periods, commas, and paragraphs, and the medium that eventually allowed me to see myself as an independent agent with a unique story to tell.

Initially seeking confirmation of my burgeoning homosexuality in the words of others, I consider the pseudoscientific tomes of Edmund Bergler and Alfred Kinsey, but the former's case studies of tortured, unhappy lives and the latter's statistics have nothing to do with the desires that course through my body. I am forced to look for more arresting representations to guide my future. Abandoning the public library and inconvenient bookstore for the corner newsstand, I discover the modest physique magazines of the 1950s. Filled with well-oiled, fig-leaf-clad torsos—no match for today's perfected, unveiled gym bodies—the Grecian Guild models are all the more human because of their imperfections. Mostly they are posed alone, however, which is both a disappointment for a teenager desperately seeking images of men together in any format and an incitement to imagining their lives as lived both on the page and off. What does the jauntily worn sailor cap or beach towel casually placed on the ground suggest about what has occurred before or will follow after the photograph is snapped? I carry on silent dialogues with all my favorites and try to enter the photographed scenario so as to have my way with these mysterious icons even as I create new stories for after the shoot has ended.

Despite these efforts, I am still dissatisfied. Unable to see myself reflected in the protoclones of that era, I draw on immediate experience as the source of my first literary efforts. Electrified by the touch of Marc's hand on my shoulder as we walked home from the museum, unnerved by Roger's invitation for a sleepover date that New Year's Eve, mesmerized by the folds in Donald's electric-blue bathing suit— I begin to authorize my own life.

Now, like Jean Genet, I turn the act of writing itself into an erotic moment. Seeing my words provides an illicit pleasure that I hardly understand. Hiding nothing from myself, I spend hours secreting away my desires from others even as I hope they will be discovered. These brief, furtively written narratives are the precursors to a more formal statement, a homoerotic short story deeply indebted to my first reading of James Baldwin. Undertaken as a senior English project, this personal declaration of independence, no parental editing required, is ultimately returned by the teacher without a single comment—so much for coming out in 1960. Although I am ready and able to put my desires onto paper, albeit transformed into the lives of fictionalized characters, I speak to no one about the essay. The one person who reads it is herself left wordless. This move to represent what is inside undoubtedly functions as an effective distancing mechanism through which I can better see myself, part of the drive to get on with the inevitable. Emboldened by my imminent graduation, I use the assignment to prepare for the real coming out that will take place only weeks after I arrive at my freshman dorm at college.

As I become a writer, I also become a reader. In his short but memorable essay "On Reading," Proust describes the places and days in which he first became absorbed by books. What remains most vivid about childhood reading, he claims, is not the text itself but the call to an early lunch when the chapter is not quite finished, the summer outing during which our only desire is to return to the book left hastily aside on the dining room table, or the secret pleasure of reading in bed long after all the adults have gone to sleep. While particular phrases titillate our curiosity and provoke our desire, Proust assures us that there is no truth to be found in words themselves, just the keys that help us to unlock interior rooms of our own design. Only in adolescence does the solitude required of the engaged reader become tolerable, dare I say attractive, to me. And only then am I able to set aside my own immediate interests to lend the book my larger life.

Although I favor long family narratives and bildungsromans with lots of character development and psychological complications, my tastes are eclectic. I am especially given to perusing my parents' bookshelves, which contain everything from Kafka's *Metamorphosis*, forbidden to my best friend by his more protective parents, to Ayn Rand's *The Fountainhead* and Oscar Wilde's *Ballad of Reading Gaol*. I have no interest in lightweight subjects such as the thirty-five-cent Signet edition mysteries that my father reads on the train to work each day and then jams into his raincoat pocket. Once stacked high in separate piles around the house—my father is a fast reader—they eventually begin to disappear, replaced by my mother's ever-growing library of hardcover fiction.

Now, on the very same shelves, wedged in between books on Jewish history and biographies of Zionist leaders (my father's) and piled haphazardly atop an assortment of art books (my mother's) are the volumes containing my own essays on education. I have never become used to seeing them mixed in with the volumes of my childhood; they seem oddly out of context, misplaced fragments from the academic world. And what do these carefully proffered "gifts" mean to my parents?

They are proud of my scholarly achievements, clearly unimagined when I announced my intention of working with young children thirty years ago. Then my parents were convinced that I had thrown away my chances at a career that would bring significant financial remuneration or public recognition. My mother always reads my essays, careful to comment on how well written they are and to acknowledge how difficult it is to follow the details of the arguments. My father is less interested in what they say about education than in what they signify about my career. Of course, the books on early childhood find a more prominent place on their coffee table than those on queer theory. So I am surprised to learn how eager my father is to send a journal article on the impact of HIV/AIDS on the gay community to my cousin's daughter who has recently come out. Needless to say, he doesn't read it himself, but the mere fact that he will traffic in once contraband matter is an indication of how far he has come in acknowledging the existence of gay and lesbian lives.

When I was thirty-four, just ten years before this request to send on my article, my father evidenced a very different attitude. We, Bob and I and my parents, have just eaten in a favorite Chinese restaurant and are walking across Eighty-sixth Street in Manhattan. It's a broad thoroughfare, bustling with pedestrian traffic and lined with clothing shops, electronics-cum-Oriental-rug outlets, and discount drug stores. My mother and Bob are in the lead while my father and I trail behind. He is already showing the first signs of the spinal stenosis and limited vision that will eventually undermine his balance completely. For now, I am only aware that he sways slightly as he walks, and I am forced closer to the buildings with every step. He cannot move in a straight line.

I am eager and a little apprehensive about sharing my news with him. I have just published my first article in a radical gay newspaper, a diatribe against mainstream political organizations. My father listens carefully to my description of the article even as I see him become increasingly upset. "But why did you have to publish *there?*" he finally blurts out. My father hates the word "gay," winces every time I use it, and would never refer to a "gay" newspaper. I explain my desire to speak to a particular audience, the community of which I am a member, and to influence the direction of the political current. Then, his anger boiling over, he asks the question that goes to the heart of our muddled relationship, "And why did you have to use *my* name?"

I am stunned by this of all responses and caught totally caught off guard. It feels as if I have been punched in the stomach and I am breathless. Naively I had wanted to gain my father's approval by announcing myself a published author, an adult who might influence the thinking of others. Instead, he suddenly makes me feel like a shamed child who has stolen something inviolable, his father' name. In his eyes I am not a separate, autonomous adult but a dependent child, an extension of his ego, who has failed to request permission to grow up. My life is conditional, contingent upon his approval.

We continue walking in silence. "But Dad," I finally stammer, "I never thought about using a pseudonym. I am proud of my article." More silence. I can feel his fierce, unrelenting anger, a father betrayed by his own son. I try to fill the void again with a more practical suggestion that again misses the mark. "Dad, remember," I offer, "that the *Gay Community News* is a very small Boston paper and that, if any of your acquaintances should read it, they are most likely gay themselves." Still no response.

While I anticipated his discomfort with my public identification as a gay person and the potential harm to which I might be exposed, I did not foresee my father's sense of personal injury and the shadow my gayness casts over his life. I am shocked to realize that he fears more for himself than for me. While I have long been aware of the paranoid temperament that makes my father loath to reveal any but the most benign information to others, I didn't realize that he would feel directly contaminated, perhaps threatened, by my gayness. So now I am driven by a child's need for parental approval to say the painful and the obvious, "Dad, you know it's my name too. It's true that I never thought about the repercussions that publishing in an obscure gay newspaper might have for you. But what would you expect me to do? I have no intention of hiding and every desire to participate in a larger public world." By now we have caught up to Bob and my mother, and it's clear that my father has said all that he can or is willing to say.

Our conversation is brief, but its impact long lasting. My father's desire to control my use of "his" name reflects the confused boundaries and emotional intensity that characterize our relationship. Once again, it is words that bind us together and keep us apart. My father's response also confirms what I have long suspected: my resistance to reading and my difficulties mastering the basics of composition mirrored an intuitive understanding that the written word would lead me to new places, on my own, away from the protective sheltering of my family. Always given to severe attacks of homesickness as a child, I neither wanted to venture forth nor, once pushed forward by others, to be surrounded by reminders of the people and places that I had left behind. Reading and writing still carry an emotional resonance tinged with these fears of separation from and desires for my father. This resonance, the feeling of alienation and homesickness, has never been more powerful than now, as I write to assert the continuation of my life in the face of his death.

Over time, my parents have learned to take some pride in my career, which has been built on subjects that once seemed more a source of private shame than a cause for public discourse. They have come to recognize that throughout my work on young children, HIV/AIDS, and gay/lesbian life, there is a consistent interest in creating a more equitable society. While never politically active, they understand this demand for social justice as a matter of ethics, for what, in the Jewish tradition, has been called *tikkun olam*, or repair of the world.

As a teacher and researcher I am all too familiar with the post-modern literature that declares a crisis of representation in the humanities and social sciences. Is it possible or even desirable to be objective when describing the lives of others? What if informants disagree with our interpretations of their lives? What if the "other" is a loved one or parent?

While I have studied this theoretical literature at length, attended endless conference presentations, and spent hours in debate with colleagues, I am woefully unprepared for the personal crisis that occurs while writing my first book. Depicting the death from AIDS of my San Francisco boyfriend, Michael, I obsess about my ability to capture his life in words. A commanding and powerful writer himself, would he approve my efforts? Would he contest them? I tell myself that I am writing my own story as much as his and that I am not benefiting from his death but using our experience in the interests of education, of children, and of other people with HIV/AIDS. I rely on his profound understanding of the political, his engaging sense of humor, and Zen sensibility to conjure up his consent to my project.

The actual publication of the book precipitates yet another crisis as I consider how people who know Bob will respond to the portrayal of my deep attachment to Michael and the terrible grief I experience at his death. Bob and I have never been monogamous and in this sense our lives mirror those of many gay people who have constructed a culture in which erotic pleasures and intimate attachments are not constrained by traditional mores. A revelation of this sort in a memoir is not unusual, and it is often the stuff of great fiction. But people who write books about early childhood curriculum aren't expected to describe the complexity of their domestic arrangements, especially if they involve same-sex love. While privately many gay people express gratitude for my frankness, in public arenas nothing is said. Academic decorum or simple denial? Perhaps those made uncomfortable by my work simply stay far away, dismissing it as irrelevant or self-referential.

A similar silence falls over my parents with respect to the stories about Michael and my gay adolescence that appear in the book. They never ask about these narratives, not even the final one in which my father metaphorically stands by my side as I stand for Michael at the gay synagogue during Yizkor, the memorial service for the dead. Did he even read it? Nor does my mother's almost complete absence from the text give rise to the recriminations I worried about. Did she even notice it?

I suspect that with the passage of time from my first *Gay Community News* article, my parents came to terms with my sexual orientation and the role it plays in my public/professional life. This process did not involve extensive dialogue with me but it did resolve the anger and resentment expressed earlier by my father. Like many other parents of gay children, my father and mother must have arranged an emotional boundary between their feelings about "homosexuality" more generally and their continuously loving disposition toward me. It was not until their own physical decline set in, however, that they experienced directly the kindness and care that endeared Bob to them. I am not sure that my parents could *love* anyone who was not flesh and blood, but I do know that their tolerance and acceptance eventually turned into the deep appreciation that characterized their later relationship with him.

These concerns that shadowed my first book soon begin to pale when I start to write essays in which my parents themselves are central characters. Weighing my feelings of guilt about hiding something from them against my fear of the blame they will heap upon me for misrepresenting their lives, initially I decide not to show them anything. How will they respond to reading that they are dying, that I am resentful of the demands their care places on me, that I see them as pathetic and helpless? I am quickly becoming the kind of writer/researcher that I have scorned in the past, the kind who does not involve the informants or share the results of his work with them.

I always seek to build collaborative relationships when conducting research. For example, studying the work of staff developers, I lead regular focus groups with them. Before each new session, I hand out a written summary of the prior meeting in order to elicit their feedback. Am I representing them accurately? Have I misunderstood their intentions? These collaborative strategies are practical; I want to conduct research that is meaningful to the participants and that helps them to look at their experience in new ways. These strategies are also ethical; I want to minimize the distortions and judgments to which outsiders are given in describing the experience of others. Sometimes, however, political considerations interfere.

One such politically charged effort at collaborative research stands out for me. I have spent three weeks anticipating the meeting with the college president to discuss the distribution of our report on the school-reform project. Given the difficult politics in the school district, do we want to release a report that is highly critical of the current change efforts and that documents the ongoing mistreatment of children and adults in the system? Will we lose our place at the table of reform? Will our adversaries in the district use the report, which is also self-critical, against us?

I am a few minutes late when I enter the president's office. An administrative foul-up has required that the meeting be held an hour earlier than expected. Slightly out of breath, irritated by the change of time, and hoping to keep my impulse to speak too quickly in check, I am surprised when a women turns to me saying, "We haven't really started. We were waiting for you." Although I am one of a handful of men in the college and the only man on this project with a staff of twenty-five, I am suddenly struck by being the only male in the room of five female executives. Can they have been waiting for me to lay out the agenda? I don't want to be the dominating male, although this is unlikely, given that the president is always well prepared and is known to have done an especially close reading of the report. Concerned about how the college represents itself to the larger educational public, she questions whether our ethnographic approach to research will convince elected officials and funders of the value of our work. In the age of educational standards and intensified testing, what kind of research will be most effective in helping others to understand the benefits of progressive education?

While some in the room express hesitations about the impact of the report on our future relations with the school district, my overriding concern is our commitment to the teachers and staff who have told us their stories and which we have tried to represent. Our obligation, I volubly argue, is to them, and our ability to continue telling their stories will be severely compromised if we withhold the report from wide-scale circulation. I say that if teachers and staff feel that they have been misrepresented, then we must bear the consequences. A consensus for widespread distribution builds as the meeting ends.

On the inside I participate in a very different dialogue. For I am only too aware that in other contexts, I am much less confident, unwilling to accept the imagined consequences of sharing my documentation projects. Where my parents are involved, practical and ethical considerations give way under the weight of the emotional baggage I bring to researching their lives and mine.

In need of validation, I send my essays to two cousins with explicit instructions not to share them with other family members. I am only too happy for strangers to read these ruminations on aging, but the more people who know my parents read the essays, the deeper my feelings of disrespect. One cousin advises me to show them the work. She says that she would be proud to have children who write so lovingly about her. But she speaks as a sixty-year-old at the height of her powers, not as a fragile eighty-seven-year-old near the end of life. I don't believe she knows what it has been like for me to be the perennial target of blame, the container of so much parental anger and anxiety. Nor is this a role I ever anticipated playing in my parents' life. Indeed it is only in 1990, at age forty-five, that I have my first insight into the nature of the drama that I am destined to participate in.

My father is undergoing risky and complicated surgery to save the sight in his one good eye. My mother, my aunt, and I are waiting for him when he returns from the operation. Only local anesthetic is used during such surgeries, and my father lies fully awake but motionless in the bed. My mother and aunt hover over the patient, trying to make him comfortable. I stand at a distance. Suddenly I hear him call out my name in terror, declare the operation a failure, and blame me for having allowed it to happen. My father believes that he is permanently blind because he can't see anything at all. A surgical patch, which will be removed in twenty-four hours, covers his good eye. I am paralyzed and cannot respond. My own vision is beginning to blur. I feel dizzy and unsteady on my feet. As my father continues to wail in despair, my mother tries to calm him. I slip out of the room and find a seat on a window ledge in the hallway. I place my head between my legs as I have been taught to do in these situations, but the dizziness continues. I can hear my father calling my name. My aunt, thinking I haven't heard his cries, comes to get me. Still overwhelmed and unable to stand, I tell her that I will return as quickly as I can. But it is ten minutes before I am composed enough to take my father's hand and reassure him that in fact the operation is a success and that he will have his sight back the following day. Once he is quieted, he reassures me that he is not in pain. We both marvel at his report of being able to overhear the doctor's talking during the operation and to feel the pressure of their tools resting on his chest as they proceeded with the delicate procedure. By the time he is ready to doze off, I am exhausted too.

I leave with my father's cries ringing in my ears. I am ashamed by my inability to respond. Since my father does not have tubes leading to and from his body, I know it is the emotion of the moment, not the sight of medical paraphernalia that has caused me to black out. But what is the emotion of the moment? Am I frightened for him or for myself? It feels like I absorb my father's cries directly into my body. I am defenseless against his panic, at the same time as I am named as its cause—"I told you I shouldn't have the operation. I knew it was too risky. Why did I listen to you?" Sucked into the maelstrom of his emotions, I am unable to swim to the shore of rationality or to throw him the flimsiest buoy of reassuring words to which he might cling. My father feels himself to be the helpless victim and has tried to make me one too.

I wondered then, and continue to wonder now, why it was me and not my mother who he called, who he blamed, and who he ultimately trusted to tell him the truth.

My father's feelings of betrayal are justified. Not because I used his name in my articles on gay politics or because I recommended the operation he thought had failed, but because I am claiming new powers as he has difficulties retaining old ones. And above all, because I will live and he will soon die. Asserting my difference at the exact moment when he needs me to be the same, to protect him from the onslaught of old age, my father lashes out with a fundamental emotional truth. Betrayal is at the heart of our relationship. I have abandoned him, refusing the identification that he thinks would ensure his future.

In fact, I left my parents' house long ago, during my early twenties, when I realized that my survival depended on constructing a life far away from the emotional morass in which they lived and through which they tried to control their children. Although I know this rejection was a source of deep pain for them, I have no regrets. Now that I have been drawn me back into their world, the conflicts that were packed away in old cedar chests, the resentments left hanging in upstairs closets, the ambivalence buried in basement storage bins are revisited. The demands of the present don't leave much time for such musings, and I am suspicious of nostalgia anyway. I move forward by generating fresh texts and by giving life to new stories. It's a confusing enterprise, however, for the process of separation is occurring at the same time as moments of the closest physical connection—when a dry mouth must be swabbed with a glycerin stick, a feeding tube filled with sustenance, a soiled diaper changed. Even as I write to differentiate myself, to leave them behind, I assure my continuing connection. After all, they have become both the subject matter without which I cannot work and from which I hope to free myself.

Yet at times I can't help but agree with Nancy K. Miller who, in *Bequest and Betrayal*, describes her own effort to write about her father as the ultimate act of bad faith. In the Jewish tradition we are commanded to bear witness and to remember. At the very same time, however, we are asked to honor the biblical injunction not to look upon our father's naked body, to respect his privacy. We are caught between contradictory demands. Writing the details of his life offers revenge for the wounds that he has inflicted, continues to inflict. In answer to the exposure that his death threatens, I make him vulnerable in my texts. He is needy, childlike, out of control. He is egocentric, thankless, and without remorse. I write suspended between anger, with its risk of mandatory repetition, and compassion, with its potential for idealization.

I lie to my parents when they ask about my work. My gerontologist friend would call it a therapeutic lie. I tell them that I am writing about childhood. "Is it about, you know, that homosexual stuff?" my father probes. He still can't use the word "gay," and when he says "homosexual," it sounds remote and forced. Hearing that he is detached but not disdainful, I take a deep breath and venture a little closer to the truth. "Well, dad, you know that I am writing about my own childhood, and so it's got to include some gay stuff. Everything I write has something in it about being gay." Tempted to go further, the gay stuff no longer the stumbling block, I wait silently for more questions, but none come. Like the good sex educator, I try to give enough information to satisfy his curiosity but not more than is actually being requested. Mine is a sin of omission.

At home again, I seek reassurance. On the shelf just above my desk, I find the purple-jacketed hardcover edition of Ruth Behar's *The Vulnerable Observer*. Recommended two years previously by a close colleague, it has retained a place of primacy on top of my all-important stack of recently read books. A committed feminist and anthropologist, Behar intertwines her own stories—the death of her grandparents—with those of the people she studies—the mourning rituals of a village in southern Spain. She unashamedly writes to make sense of her own life as much as to understand larger social phenomena. I am deeply moved by her work. She encourages me as I struggle to write about my parents and childhood, my life, and the schools that I visit regularly.

It is a young student who, noticing a connection between Behar's work and my own, refers me to an essay that at this moment confirms my decision not to talk further with my parents. Here Behar reveals the bitter enmity she endured from her father upon the publication of her first book, *Translated Woman*. None of her insights into the complex ways that personal and professional stories intersect make any difference to her parents. Like my own father twenty years ago, her father rails against the way she dishonors *his* name. Unlike my father's complaints, his are specific. She has written that that he is ashamed of his own father, a poor peddler in Cuba. She has described how he vindictively destroyed the letters she wrote him while away at college. She airs the family's dirty linen in public as a way to get back at him, spiteful revenge. Her mother, whom Behar has taken the liberty of referring to as a typist rather than using her full title of Diploma Aide, comes to the point, "Mira, I'm going to tell you something, Rutie . . . 'La mierda no se revuelve, porque apesta. Don't stir up the shit, because it will stink.'" Unable to resolve the difficulties with her parents, relations remain strained. Behar decides not to share her writing or the nature of her professional life with them in the future.

Why do we write? Who do we imagine will read the text? How do we know that we have represented others responsibly? I worked in the school-reform project for three years before writing anything other than the official documents required of our formal evaluation. I fulfilled my professional responsibilities while remaining at a distance, my feelings kept closely under wraps. I told myself that many others had already described the urban decay, social dislocation, and racism I was witnessing. What could I say that hadn't been said before? If Jean Anyon's carefully documented history of school corruption, Jonathan Kozol's biting description of the savage inequalities in American education, and Valerie Polakow's heartrending ethnography of children growing up in the Other America hadn't brought about change, why would my writing be any more effective?

Eventually I began to suspect, however, that the emotional detachment with which I went about my work, the much-vaunted stance of scientific objectivity that I assumed, and my reluctance to tell our project's story were not so much a tribute to what others had already seen and written as a defensive maneuver against what I was feeling. I simply wasn't strong enough to become a vulnerable observer in poor urban schools. Behar argues that such personal vulnerability is required to successfully enter another culture, to become aware of how our own histories are reflected in what we see and what we don't see, what we choose to report as "data" and what we choose to call irrelevant, "beyond the limits of this study." By going beyond the limits of traditional studies, we seek to engage the adult reader in the way Proust reminds us that young people can be engaged in an absorbing work of fiction. But for social scientists the pleasures of the text alone will not suffice. So we risk the personal and the confessional to highlight the social and the political in the hope of moving others to action.

In contrast, from the first days of my mother's hospitalization, I did not hesitate to record my thoughts and feelings. I scribbled notes on the late-night bus home from New York City and early in the morning before beginning work. Although, once these notes began to accumulate and my file folders to expand, I had paralyzing reservations about how to organize them into a larger narrative. I did not see my parents' story as unique. Nightly conversations with friends were now filled with diatribes about the refusal of parents to accept help from adult children, the complexity of their care, and guilt about our inability to do enough. Despite the fact that I could not imagine an audience interested in such concerns, I continued to write.

Sometimes I felt myself drowning in the vast sea of my parents' practical and emotional needs. Although I knew I would be a better caregiver with a stronger defense mechanism in place, I could not find a more distanced perspective from which to view their situation. At the same time, I wondered how my work as an educational researcher might change if my emotions were less tied up in the knot of my parents' final years. I don't believe we have some finite amount of emotional energy or that my experiences with poor, minority children and my white, middle-class family are equivalent. Their very real discomforts aside, my parents are receiving the best care possible in the setting of their choice, the apartment they have lived in for forty years. The wrath of my father is the wrath of a man who remains ambitious for himself and for his children, not the wrath of a man who has directly suffered social injustice.

In the schools I visit there are too many children whose basic health and educational needs aren't being met and too many teachers who have little or no control over their professional lives. The contexts that I move between and the potential remedies to ameliorate the problems I observe couldn't be more different. In one I am the ultimate outsider—a white, Jewish, highly educated male, part of an effort to change poor/working-class elementary schools populated by African American and Latino children. In the other I am the ultimate insider, the son who bears responsibility for his aging parents. Nevertheless, I have become curious about the ways that these disparate experiences live within me.

Each is a story of loss, and as Ruth Behar suggests, we can only write them with "an awareness of how excruciating are the paradoxes of attachment and displacement." I grieve for the lives that my parents have lived, for my own childhood, and for the belief in immortality that will ultimately be pierced by their death. At the same time, I grieve for the lives that many children in poor urban schools won't live, for the missed opportunities to teach meaningful lessons about education, social change, and personal efficacy, and for the coherent communities that once existed in the today's fragmented neighborhoods. Both projects demand that I bear witness to the suffering of others and that I be absolutely pitiless with myself.

I try not to give in to hopelessness. I resist the rescue fantasy that seduces me into believing that I can prevent my parents from further pain, even death, and that the educational reforms we propose will change the life prospects of the children in our project's classrooms. I replace the lure of rescue with the reality of living alongside another. And I struggle to make sense of what is happening within me and those I write about, between my life as caregiver and my life as researcher. For I have come to believe that it is in these awkward spaces and unexpected relationships that I may just find a story that hasn't been told before.

6

Unspoken Subjects

> Once *home* was a far away place, I had never
> been to but knew well out of my mother's mouth.
> She breathed exuded hummed the fruit smell
> of Noel's Hill morning fresh and noon hot, and
> I spun visions of sapadilla and mango as a net
> over my Harlem tenement cot in the snoring
> darkness rank with nightmare sweat.
> AUDRE LORDE, *Zami: A New Spelling of My Name*

When I was growing up, my parents did not speak longingly of another time and place. There was no mythology to master and little
poetry to imbibe. As Jews of Eastern European descent, we were heirs
to a tradition that more often reminded me of dark, cramped shtetl
rooms with hard wooden benches for Talmudic study than lush, sun-
filled days in tropical settings. We lived in a permanent Diaspora, yet
I never really believed myself to be in exile or that my parents wished
to be elsewhere. Of course there was always the ritual singing at the
close of the Passover Seder—"Next year in Jerusalem!"—signaling
that our true home was only to be found in Israel. My primary sense of
connection was to an overbearing intellectual heritage, peppered on

occasion with the domestic humor of *Yidishkayt*, not to a rich spiritual life or one that promised sensuous pleasures of the body.

I will never know if the fact that my grandmothers were sisters had anything to do with it. But they both married men who were serious scholars, active in the Jewish community, and successful in the "dry goods" business. They personified a certain time period, a wave of Jewish immigrants who placed an exceedingly high value on learning for themselves and for their children. I can't imagine that my grandparents were disappointed in the large number of Ivy League diplomas and advanced degrees amassed by their offspring during the 1920s and 1930s, who in turn sustained similar ideas about the value of education.

Needless to say, when I dropped out of Harvard in the early 1960s and was in serious doubt about my own commitment to scholarship, my parents were deeply troubled. This was the time, when I was on the cusp of adulthood, that my father spoke most vividly about his own father. The talks were infused with the significance of intellectual projects for Jews who lived a transient existence, subject to devastating pogroms, and always at risk for imminent exile. Perhaps too recent and too overwhelming, the Holocaust itself was never mentioned. I was reassured that the life of the mind could not be confiscated and would travel well if necessary. Underpinning this history lesson, but mostly unspoken, was the middle-class assumption that degrees in the pocket—postgraduate work a necessity—had the power to provide financial security and social status.

Despite my father's reluctantly offered lectures on anti-Semitism during these years, and the emphasis on expressing feelings and fears in my younger days, like most of my peers, I grew up in a household filled with silences. Later, as a young adult, I was determined to break through these silences, writing a master's essay on the place of death education in the classroom. Then, as a gay man and HIV/AIDS educator during the 1980s, I became an advocate for socially relevant curriculum for even the youngest children. With these consuming passions, I fell prey to a particular form of amnesia about the secrets that framed my childhood.

Then one chilly fall night in 1999, on my way home from my parents' apartment, I found myself on the northeast corner of Eighty-sixth Street and Fifth Avenue and noticed that a work shed had grown up around the ornate limestone and red-brick mansion that had long stood on the southeast corner. Seeing the shed, I recalled a short article in the *New York Times* announcing that the YIVO Institute for Jewish Research, the building's last occupant, was moving to a modern facility in Chelsea where it would join forces with another archive of Jewish history. It was a time of cultural mergers as well as corporate takeovers. Drained by my efforts to shore up my parents' own sagging prospects, I saw that the massive metal and glass front doors of the once grand but always graceless building were boarded over with plywood, a harsh fluorescent bulb was giving off an eerie light on the first floor, and the tall French windows on the second floor had been carelessly left open.

A preservationist with a deep longing for the city of the 1940s in which I grew up, distressed by the disappearance of familiar structures, even those of no particular architectural value, I viewed the gutting of the former YIVO Institute with a mixture of dread and relief. For while it reminded me of a disquieting childhood visit to this former repository of Jewish memory, it also suggested the possibility of deconstructing that visit, which has haunted my adult life.

It is 1954. I am ten years old, and unlike many of my friends from liberal and well-assimilated homes, I attend Hebrew school with great enthusiasm. Engaged by the challenge of learning a second language and enjoying instruction in ritual practices, I am considered by the teachers to be a model student despite my poor reading skills and total ignorance of the rules of English grammar. On this particular Sunday morning, we are taking a field trip, the only one in all my years of attendance at the Society for the Advancement of Judaism. I can't recall either a prior announcement of the trip nor any discussion of what we were to see before crowding onto the city bus that would take us directly across the park to the YIVO.

It's all slightly shabby; those large, high-ceilinged rooms with elaborate wood paneling and heavy, faded red draperies to shield the display cases from direct sunlight were expensive to maintain even then, I suppose. Here is memorabilia from shtetl life and the thriving Yiddish culture of eastern Europe: diaries and letters, Torahs and tallisim, Kiddush cups and prayer books. Like the upstairs rooms, the basement exhibit areas are cool and dark, but the space has low ceilings and is cramped. It feels completely utilitarian. And in these display cases are the infamous bars of soap made from the ash of concentration camp crematoria, the lampshades made from the stretched skin of inmates, and the photographs of emaciated children and adults with shaven heads, bare feet, and striped pajamas either too big or too small for even these skeletal bodies. We move from case to case, our small group of eight or nine huddled together, understanding and not understanding all at the same time. Our teacher, a tall, attractive, middle-aged Sabra, whose son is in the Israeli army and who becomes anxious with the news of every border skirmish, is beside us. I don't know what she is thinking. She isn't saying anything, at least anything I can recall.

I remember that morning as a profoundly disturbing introduction to the methodical and mundane practices of the Third Reich. The collections of wedding rings, gold fillings, and eyeglasses tell me that attention was paid to the very last detail. The pictures of German soldiers and SS officers, the former in long woolen army coats and the latter in black leather, rounding up civilians in city streets, tell me that there was little chance of escape. Other photographs, of people clutching suitcases and children, anxiously waiting to be transported or arriving at final destinations, lined up sometimes clothed and sometimes totally naked, make the abstract and unimaginable graphically real. Trying to regulate the impact of these images, I neither look directly at them nor turn completely away. I don't understand my relationship to these people who appear so different from me and oc-

cupy such bleak, threatening landscapes. Beyond the identifying label, Jew, what can we possibly have in common? Surely I will not
share the same fate. I am frightened into a silence that makes it impossible, even today, to find the right words to describe my confusing
emotions. Can there be right words? How can something that is such
a muddle be so important?

At times I wonder if my memories of the YIVO are to be trusted.
They are powerful and unsettling. They are hazy and lack detail. Perhaps I have imbued this early experience with images and feelings acquired later. Perhaps the dreams in which I am on my own, hiding in
strange apartments, running through ominous city streets, seeking
anonymity in large, open train sheds, and waking up just moments before capture by the Gestapo, are the result of too many war movies,
not my YIVO visit. Perhaps they date from a trip to Munich at age
eighteen when I was overwhelmed by the sounds of the German language coming from loudspeakers on busy train platforms and read every face for indications of anti-Semitism. Can the YIVO be only an
emblem, a container into which I have poured emotions and images
collected in other places, at other times? The murky pool of memories
that I draw on gives rise to strong emotions but few explanations.

Eventually the YIVO building was transformed into the elegant
Neue Galerie Museum for German and Austrian Art. Unspoken during my adolescence was another connection to the YIVO, with its origins in Vilna circa 1925, its governing board that included Sigmund
Freud, and its relocation to New York during World War II. Vilna,
then part of Lithuania, had a thriving intellectual life and was the
very same city from which my father's father had immigrated decades
before. Now in New York, my family had found itself just two blocks
from a venerable Jewish archive with its roots in the same physical
and cultural geography.

As I wait on the corner that night looking at the former YIVO building, reexperiencing that troubling Sunday morning visit, I also realize
how, over the years, I have watched my parents' participation in Jew-

ish life decline. Recently, every suggestion that they visit a neighboring synagogue has been gently but firmly rebuffed. Neither of my parents will be seen in a wheelchair. This reflects a self-defeating pride as well as fear of drawing attention to themselves. My mother's resistance is not surprising, as her Jewish commitments have clearly always revolved around home and family, holidays and celebrations, rather than the synagogue. Memories of my father, however, tell another story of a fuller religious life, a life that I hoped would offer some succor in these last difficult years.

As a young man my father was observant, rising early every morning to say prayers, bound in tefillin, the small phylacteries containing sacred texts. When his mother died he went to shul each morning for an entire year, as traditional practice demands. I was six at the time and remember seeing him return to the house on weekdays when I was just getting up for breakfast. On some weekend mornings I accompanied him to the imposing sanctuary where a small group of men were gathered to fulfill their commitments. Most vivid were the Friday nights when I was called to the front of the shul to participate in one ceremony or another. Gripped by fear, pushed forward by my father, I had no idea what was expected of me or why I was being singled out. The honor for the father was only an anxious moment for the son.

After the official year of mourning was over, my father would attend services on holidays and occasionally on weekends. Despite his limited formal participation in synagogue life, he was recognized within our larger family circle not only for his ability to chant the Hebrew prayers with speed and authority but also for the confidence with which he knew his away around the prayer book.

I wonder what happened to my father's religious feelings during his last years. Has he lost faith, become cynical? Or, like many modern Jews, are his primary commitments to a particular culture and historical identity? Were public practices always secondary to privately held beliefs?

Although my father is more tied to traditional rituals than is my mother, perhaps the core of his religious life is not so different. This is to say that he too experiences religion mainly as a vehicle for affirming family ties. The ever-dutiful son, the year of mourning is homage to his mother, to doing the right thing. With her death, my father becomes the emotional and practical center of life among his five siblings. Some call nightly and some less regularly. During his seventies and well into his eighties he is the primary caregiver to his youngest and eldest sisters through prolonged illnesses. I imagine that there may well be a reparative quality to this caregiving, a way that my father can make up for his desertion of the family as a young man when he married my mother and moved to New York.

My father is ruled by an overbearing superego; his ability to forgive others, although never himself, helps to explain why so many seem to rely on him. He is an empathetic listener, and before dementia sets in, his responses are seldom ego driven. A realist who allows people to assess their options, my father is seldom critical of actions already taken by others. Intentions rather than outcomes dominate his thinking and assessments of behavior. His ultimate concerns are ethical rather than spiritual.

The trip to the YIVO in 1954 does not dampen my enthusiasm for Hebrew school or make me doubt that I am Jewish. It does, however, complicate matters. I am less clear about what being Jewish means. I wonder what "their" terrible history in eastern Europe has to do with my present. Why does such a catastrophe occur? Can it happen here? Most important, there are no further opportunities to make sense out of the fragments of information we managed to glean that day.

Before the YIVO, we children of middle-class Jewry know with varying degrees of certainty that something terrible happened in Germany during the war. But the emphasis is on the war itself, the Americans and other Allies against the Germans. Like the Japanese, the Germans are villains, but, because they are also Caucasians, they are not dehumanized in quite the same way. The "yellow peril" is always an external threat, so "other" that it can never be inside of us. But German aggression is all the more scary because they are like us, can be us, or we can be them. Indeed, my nurse, who worked for various family members over the years, is German, a source of considerable confusion when I am young. I cannot understand the possibility of being German, the enemy, and Jewish at the same time. Later, studying the Israeli struggle for independence, identifying the enemy continues to be a difficult task. It is incomprehensible that an American ally, the mild-mannered English who speak the same language, are now to be despised, the target of our own Jewish aggression.

After the YIVO, there are only infrequent and disconnected references to the fate of the Jews in Europe, but all this lacks the coherence of what is now referred to as the Holocaust. Then there were discrete nouns—concentration camp, ghetto, gas chamber—but no verbs with which to connect them into a meaningful narrative. A label, a story with beginning, middle, and end, offers a handle on events, and this is an event still too hot to be handled, a fire burning so brightly you can't look directly into it.

Above all, my parents want to see themselves as modern and forward thinking. Our apartment is filled with 1930s clean-lined furniture of their own design, George Jensen silverware, and gray Russell Wright dishes that match the walls. My mother's social work training encourages a hypersensitivity to psychological states and my father's undergraduate career at Harvard has put him in touch with a world far larger than that of the small, western Pennsylvania town into which he was born. When they marry there is no question but that my parents will live in New York City and raise a family away from the potential anti-Semitic slurs that so painfully punctuated my father's early life. The anonymity of urban life is what my mother knows and my father craves.

As do other parents of their era, my mother and father practice protectiveness toward their children with respect to talking about tough topics such as race, poverty, or war. The silence is cultural as well as embedded in the scientific research about childhood. My mother reads Sigmund Freud as part of her education in the 1930s, although it is not for another decade that she will have access to Anna

Freud and Dorothy Burlingham's groundbreaking clinical work with war orphans in England to bolster her natural reserve. While calling attention to the fears and anxieties aroused by real deprivations and losses, Freud and Burlingham suggest that most young children are more damaged than helped by too close an examination of the aggression expressed in adult life. That is, real hostilities in the outside world are often interpreted in terms of imagined conflicts in the child's inner world. The child's inability to sort out fantasy and reality can lead to unhealthy outcomes. Because young children are vulnerable to such confusions, they need protection from the potentially disturbing knowledge of the violence practiced by individuals and nations.

When I question my parents, then in their eighties, they deny knowing very much about what was happening in Germany. The news was spotty and vague. To them, the defining historical event of their lives is not the Holocaust but the Depression and the more immediate threat it posed to survival. During the war they are absorbed by the demands of raising a young family. Afterward, like so many other Jews, my parents want to put the past behind them. And if they have questions about how to address recent events, they receive little guidance from their synagogue. For here they will only find the general admonition never to forget, along with the injunction never to become the victim again.

In Hebrew school we read stories of resistance such as that of Hannah Senesh, the teenage freedom fighter of the Warsaw ghetto. The focus is always forward, on nurturing the young if very fragile state of Israel, on the new life that had been born from the terrible destruction of the war. We save our nickels and dimes to buy trees in Israel so we can be part of this great miracle, literally making the desert bloom. From the synagogue pulpit the rabbi regularly lectures about the ethics of living in the Diaspora, a word that I hear over and over again but never understand. Even today, so strong are my childhood associations with this mysterious word that, despite its omnipresence in postcolonial theory, I continue to believe that it only applies to the

Jews. The rabbi works hard to balance the intense emotional and practical investment in the state of Israel that is expected of us—every service ends with the singing of the national anthem of Israel—with the safe and prosperous life we enjoy in America. Perhaps his sermons speak to the ambivalence of the adults, but as child I am left on my own to reconcile what I know of the history learned at the YIVO, the fledgling country that is to redeem it, and my daily experience of home and school.

Within my own family the silence about the "Holocaust" is almost complete. The fear of the stranger, even when Jewish, is so strong that we are not introduced to the idea of "survivors," let alone children of survivors. What we know about are refugees whom we are taught to feel very sorry for. The large apartment across the hall from our own functions as a rooming house for elderly if respectable-looking men and women from Germany and eastern Europe. Although I have no interest in the political and personal struggles that bring them to our West End Avenue building, I am intrigued by their domestic arrangements, which are so clearly different from our own. When the front door is ajar, I can see just far enough inside to determine that the large foyer has been turned into a dining area with cream-colored carpeting. A vaguely oriental vase sits atop a stately oval table of dark mahogany. As the residents come and go, they greet each other with what I recognize as profusely polite but totally unintelligible phrases. Later, in the privacy of my own room, I spend hours shamelessly imitating these strange guttural languages.

Far more forbidding are the inhabitants of the ground-floor apartment facing the street, a location that I instinctively recognize to be déclassé. While the three generations of nearly indistinguishable women dressed entirely in black clearly compose a family, they seem far more foreign than our seventh-floor neighbors. Are they in perpetual mourning? Why are there no men? Occasionally I catch a glimpse of a girl my own age or slightly younger as she enters or leaves the building, but I never hear any of the severe and forbidding adults say a word. In our comfortably middle-class world these particular refugees seem to be doubly displaced persons, persons in transit, unable or unwilling to make accommodation to this temporary stopping point.

Mostly I remember the kindly older couple who own the modest candy shop that is a favorite childhood haunt. They patiently endure my twice-weekly visits that always include an exhaustive inventory of their stock. Although very small, the shop's floor-to-ceiling shelves are filled with boxes of elegantly wrapped imported chocolates. The display cases are similarly overloaded with containers of candied fruits, assorted nuts, and trays of freshly baked cookies. Enticing as all these are, irrevocably influenced by my German nurse, I am inevitably drawn to the displays of marzipan, artfully crafted to resemble fruits, vegetables, sandwiches, and my favorite—a hot dog in a bun. Just as inevitable too is the day that I notice the row of numbers and letters tattooed on the forearm of one of the owners. Is it revealed as the husband stretches for the blue and white tin of Swiss chocolates on a shelf too high for my mother to reach? Or is it the hot summer day when his wife abandons the long-sleeved blouse and sweater she usually wears for a sleeveless dress?

I don't talk with my parents about this observation, but I eventually realize that disfigurement is part of being a refugee, an unlucky person who comes from the far side of Europe. I cannot fathom how Jews got to such an inhospitable part of the world in the first place, why they stayed, and, most importantly, what they have to do with me. Might I become the unthinkable, a refugee living in reduced circumstances, missing parts of my family, trying to hide the marks that indicated I am among the numbered who had been sorted for living and dying? I have many unarticulated questions and little help in seeking the answers to them.

I am twelve and answers to my questions remain illusive. My first girlfriend has invited me to attend the Broadway movie premiere of *The Diary of Anne Frank* along with her mother and older sister. Although Beth is physically more mature and sophisticated, we had enjoyed each other's company that summer, enjoyed being one of the camp couples. Once home, however, I had not enjoyed my brother's incessant teasing or my parents' intrusive curiosity, which was piqued by Beth's Park Avenue address and her mother's reputation as a successful art gallery owner.

It's a miserable winter night, but the torrential rains do not come close to the waves of anticipatory emotion sweeping over me. Much to my embarrassment, my father insists on dropping me off at Beth's house in a taxi, a trip that under ordinary circumstances I would make on my own. Beth and her family are downstairs waiting, and to my relief it is agreed that they will take me home at the end of the evening.

I enter the theatre that night preoccupied with the logistics of a first date—arrivals and departures, demonstrations of affection and restraint, talk and silences—and am confronted on the screen with the logistics of survival—securing safe shelter, storing up food, avoiding the enemy. Undoubtedly the numbing impact of the movie is heightened by my total lack of preparation for what I am to see. But the black-and-white bleakness of those Amsterdam street scenes, the anxious fear of discovery once the Frank family goes into hiding, and, above all, the stabbing sirens of the SS police cars, become an immediate part of my world, familiar reference points that mark my understanding of the Holocaust. For an adolescent, emerging from a childhood spent listening for strange sounds under the bed and possessing parents who have deep suspicions of anyone outside our close-knit family, *The Diary of Anne Frank* matches every fear from within with a fear from without. I imagine that Beth and her sister may have cried during the movie, but all that remains for me of that night is our stunned silence when the theatre lights finally come on.

Beth and I go out on a few more dates that winter. Although she runs with a faster crowd than my own elementary school friends, it is not her lack of interest but rather my own feelings of inadequacy that cause the relationship to slip away. Beth does not return to camp that following summer, and, when next I see her five years later, she has turned into a tall, slender, and stunning woman of seventeen. Needless to say, I am still intimidated but in quite a different way.

When we are young and study history, it is always somebody else's story, another world that we learn about. Then, with the passing of the decades, suddenly we find ourselves reading about a past that we have actually lived. Each of us participates in a world that at some future point may be described, interpreted, and judged by others.

In *Lost Subjects, Contested Objects*, Deborah Britzman writes a history of Anne Frank's diary—its discovery, editing, publication, reception, and ultimate transformation into theatre and film. Now I can place my date with Beth in historical context. The sirens that punctuate my dreams can be heard within the debates about how to interpret the pages that Miep Gies and Bep Voskuijl, the two secretaries who help to keep the Franks alive for so long, find scattered across the floor of the secret annex after its discovery by the SS and Dutch Security Police. Do they, as Otto Frank suggests, tell a universal story of adolescence or are they, as the journalist Meyer Levin claims, the record of an unprecedented historical event? Does Anne speak about the perseverance of the human spirit in the face of adversity or is her voice powerfully but uniquely "the voice of six million Jewish souls"? At age twelve I am largely unmoved by the so-called universal aspects of Anne's story. I experience the movie as a Jew, frightened by the graphic images of life in hiding and ultimate discovery. I do not go on to read the diary itself at that time, nor do I knowingly see other movies about the Holocaust.

Given the strong impression left by the movie, I was surprised by my response when, several years ago, I took up the book in an attempt to exorcise my childhood demons. I was drawn to its poignantly adolescent themes—the struggle for independence, the growing self-consciousness and critique of adults, the longing for a soul mate. These have undoubtedly been heightened in the 1991 definitive edition that contains material Anne's father thought too sexually explicit or damaging to his family to be included in the original 1947 version. Two-thirds of the way through the book, my reading pace slowed to a few entries a day. I grasped the dwindling number of remaining pages between my fingers with the same sad certainty that I grasped the fate awaiting the Franks. Otto Frank and Meyer Levine were both right. The diary is of a particular time and place even as it transcends that moment through the depiction of fundamental human emotions.

When I was growing up, my parents' silences about social issues offered me many lessons about what might be said and what should remain unspoken. Foremost among the unspoken subjects is human suffering, whether caused by illness, intentional cruelty, or systemic injustice. Today, I want to make up for all that was left unsaid. My educational commitment is compensatory. Troubled memories of the YIVO, the shopkeepers with indelible numbers on their arms, the refugees who came to rest in our building, do not lead me to censorship and protectionism. Rather, they prompt consideration of how adults might create opportunities for children to talk about the difficult knowledge they acquire during their early years. Beyond the mandates of the formal curriculum or our beliefs about child development, our willingness to listen and respond to the children's lived experience is shaped by our own histories. How did we learn to manage aggression, sexuality, and sadness? What patterns of loss and recuperation, separation and dependence did we subscribe to as children? This difficult work is essential to piercing the kind of social amnesia that permeated my childhood. It is undertaken to engage children in authentic conversations about the world they will inherit and to promote their active commitment to social justice, which seemed to get such short shrift in my own upbringing.

7
The Other Side of Silence

> When we are writing and the pencil
> breaks, suddenly the content of our writing
> disappears and goes into hiding, and the
> pencil that we really did not see before
> comes out of hiding to reveal itself to us.
> T. TETSUO AOKI, "The Layered Voices
> of Teaching"

We live in a noisy world. The impatient sounds of fax and answering machines, telephone beepers and voice mail, punctuate our daily lives. There is little opportunity for silence to speak, and, when it does, we are often too busy to listen. In the summer of 1997, when I ride the bus between my home on eastern Long Island and the hospital in New York City where my father lies voiceless, I am especially aware of the intrusiveness of the new technologies. The cacophony of sounds on these weekly trips—the continuous ringing of cell phones and clicking of laptop computers, the driver's shortwave radio, the attendant's amplified words about fares and safety—is a stark contrast to the silence that reigns in my father's room.

As is often the case with cancer, the events that lead up to my father's surgery happen rapidly. I am made breathless by their speed —the mysterious first symptoms, the new doctors, and technical language replete with numbers and unpronounceable words that need to be mastered within days, and, then, the 5:50 AM bus for a final consultation with the oncologist. As I collect my parents at their apartment for the brief taxi ride uptown, my father moving slowly and cautiously, holding on to the arm of his home attendant, my mother lunges ahead in an anxiety-driven haze. As we walk up the clinic steps, the heels of her shoes make a loud slapping sound against the cement. The sound is testimony to her stubborn refusal to spend money on new, more sensible, and better fitting shoes. Her weight has dropped well below a hundred pounds, little wonder that her feet do not fill the shoes. Bob reminds her endlessly of the potential dangers of the slight heel given her precarious balance. But my mother thinks too little of herself and too much of my father to make a modest investment in her own safety.

During the long wait that morning to see Dr. Lee, my parents intermittently doze and stare into space. Finally ushered into the crowded laboratory-cum-examining-room, we try to arrange ourselves in some suitable manner. A half hour later Dr. Lee enters with an intern trailing behind. He greets my parents, whom he knows from prior visits, and barely gestures toward me when my father tries to make an introduction. After a brief examination, Dr. Lee proceeds to describe the operation in which he will remove either one or both sides of the larynx. It's easy to see that my father, who initially wanted no other doctor but the well-known head of the clinic, has already transferred his trust to Dr. Lee, his associate. Dr. Lee returns this trust by looking at my father, and only at my father, throughout the interview.

Dr. Lee talks quickly and quietly, and I am having difficulty following all that he says. Hoping to take a few notes, perhaps even slow down his rapid-fire delivery, I reach for the backpack at my feet and manage to pull out a writing pad, only to find that my pen doesn't work. No matter, for Dr. Lee never sees me struggling to organize myself and never stops talking. Feeling useless and reluctant to ask questions that might reveal my absolute ignorance about tracheotomies, shunts, voice boxes and the like, I retreat into the role of the good teacher who has invited a guest expert into his classroom. I restate the key points made by the presenter while suddenly realizing that, depending on the extent of the cancer, my father may well emerge from the operation unable to ever speak again. Dr. Lee is impatient with my attempt to process his information and snaps, "If he doesn't have the operation, soon the tumor will close off the airway and it will be impossible for him to breathe. It's not about whether your father can talk or not. You are asking the wrong question." Dr. Lee makes me feel foolish beyond words. Our exchange about speech ends in my silence. Shortly thereafter the interview is over, we all shake hands, and I promise to call on Monday with a decision about the surgery.

I can tell from my father's expression that his decision has already been made. The multiple and painful biopsies, lab tests, and examinations of the proceeding weeks, combined with Dr. Lee's certainty, have undercut his usual determination to seek a second or third opinion. The handwriting is on the wall, and there is little to be said when we return to my parents' apartment.

On the bus home that afternoon I think about how often and confidently I tell my own students that they are asking the wrong question. Usually this occurs when they seek advice about why a class situation went awry or how to intervene when children are fighting. My students quickly learn that I have less interest in how they get out of a messy lesson or how to disentangle two children than in why the situation arose in the first place. What kind of planning went into the lesson? Does the physical and social environment encourage displays of aggression?

In contrast to Dr. Lee's focus on fixing what is broken or failing, which I will be ever thankful for, I am concerned with preventing problems from arising in the first place. Yet now I often think about Dr. Lee's words. They were all right and all wrong. While he made me feel naïve and foolish, he also made me realize in a moment's time what was at stake. I wonder if he would have been quite so successful had he been less harsh. Would I be more effective if I found a gentler way to redirect my students' attention? I don't know the answers to these questions. I do know that our meeting that Saturday morning brought with it a new appreciation for how, at least in some situations, identifying the right question can be a matter of survival. Perhaps, after all, my interests in beginnings and endings, time and memory, autonomy and dependence aren't so terribly different from Dr. Lee's interests in keeping the airways free and open. A brief week later, when my mother and I say goodbye to my father before his operation, somewhere deep in the bowels of that gigantic hospital, we do not know if his larynx will be salvaged. I do know that keeping my father's airways open trumps my concerns about sustaining his voice and, as we will learn later, even concerns about swallowing food and water.

Seven hours later, seated in a sterile gray room, the youthful and considerably more relaxed Dr. Lee, still dressed in green operating suit, plastic shower cap, and tennis sneakers, patiently assures us that he has been able to save two-thirds of my father's right larynx. After three weeks of being unable to speak my father will regain a natural if somewhat sandpapery voice. (We don't know that two years on the cancer will return, necessitating the removal of his remaining larynx along with the power of speech.)

Seeing my father in the recovery room later that afternoon, still heavily sedated, lifeless and waxy yellow, the frustration of being temporarily without voice does not seem so pressing. He has weathered the operation well, and I know that he will eventually be able to speak when the shunt in his throat is removed. It is only the next morning, as I enter his room, that the full impact of his situation becomes evident to me. Angry, in fact filled with rage, he keeps trying to speak, and yet no words emerge from his mouth. Then I notice, on the bed, the first of the yellow legal pads that are to be his primary mode of communication. Written in his clearest print, all capital letters, are these instructions—GET MY SON IMMEDIATELY—followed by my phone number.

Asking my father to nod when I suggest various reasons for his distress, it quickly becomes clear to me that the room that he has been moved to, containing three other patients and no real partitions, is far too public a space for this very private, partially blind, and voiceless octogenarian. My father is not appeased by the promise of increased medical attention in this "step-up" unit designed for higher-risk patients. Phobic about germs, he has never shared a hospital room with another person before, and his current vulnerability makes his demand for another room hard for me to resist.

As I begin to negotiate with the hospital personnel for a new room, the words my father has written in my absence resonate throughout my body. Although my mother is standing by his side during this time, a position she took up over sixty years ago, he knows that her own frailties will render her ineffectual. How few words it takes for my father to communicate his panic and dependency. How unnecessary it is to speak about my responsibility.

In the weeks following the throat surgery, my father learns to communicate with gesture and pen. His needs and his discomforts take on a regular pattern. After a short while, it is easy enough to second-guess his wishes. The legal pads allow for more complex conversations. I come to accept the silence as the only way to wait out the recovery. There is little to be said.

I am not there three weeks later when the shunt is removed, and my father speaks his first words. My brother calls me from the hospital room and casually asks if I want to speak with my father. For the first time in my life, the sound of his voice brings tears to my eyes.

Sitting with my father day after day, I am aware of the complicated, changing textures of our silences. There are moments when the silence seems to create an unbridgeable gap that separates us into different worlds. There are others when it allows us to be together peacefully, without straining to make small talk or to interpret our frequently misunderstood words. Silence is a relief, a refuge in which we can be present without demanding or intruding. For me, it is a new way to express care.

I have not always appreciated the ambiguities of silence or under-stood the many different ways in which it can be read. Like many other gay people, I grew up with a heightened sensitivity to the strate-gic need for silence, for keeping my own counsel. As a child I experi-enced strong feelings of difference that were not specifically linked to longings for other boys or men, but they did contribute to a rich inner life. This link only came in early adolescence when questions of voice first became erotically charged. Then, I lived in a space defined by the tension between revealing enough to attract another and concealing enough so as not to be discovered by those who might do me harm.

As an adolescent, I learned that our silences, like our words, await the interpretation of varied reading and listening audiences. I also learned that it is often better to remain silent than to use language belying our experience. The tomes that I covertly perused in libraries and bookstores during the 1950s employed a pseudoscientific lan-guage that seemed to have no relationship to the feelings and emo-tions that pulsed through my body.

Today, even though I can choose to refer to myself as homosexual, gay, or queer, I am still painfully aware of the constraints that labels place upon us and stymied by the gap between experience and articu-lation. These reservations about language do not constitute a ratio-nale for silence. Rather, they underline an existential reality—much of human experience is unspeakable, even unimaginable. Nor are we automatically accessible to each other but must continually engage in a struggle for mutual understanding.

As an early childhood teacher in the 1960s and '70s, I was used to busy classrooms filled with the sounds of young children at work. Neither silence nor stillness seemed developmentally appropriate. Charged with the task of encouraging children to verbalize their thoughts and feelings, I did not consider that the acquisition of lan-guage is a mixed blessing. Along with the parents, I welcomed the children's use of words as an unalloyed indication of development and integration into the social world. But language also imposes order and control, culture and constraint. We seldom think about what is lost.

In *The Beast in the Nursery* Adam Phillips reminds us that linguistic competency is achieved through distancing from the preverbal self and at the cost of the rich, if chaotic, emotional life of the preschool child. Language can inhibit the new and unrehearsed, the raw and embodied expressions of ideas. While failed attempts at communication remind adults of what it is like not to talk, most often words bring safety and containment. As a teacher I thought less about how to sustain fluency between the children's spoken and unspoken lives, their words and the experiences in which they are grounded, than about how to improve verbal facility.

Later, as a newly minted assistant professor, my life was haunted by pedagogical silences gone awry. Day after terrified day, I heard my freshly disciplined, carefully chosen, graduate school words soundlessly swallowed by cavernous lecture halls. I looked out from the podium, so clearly designed for other, wiser, more charismatic instructors, to see students casually leafing through books, surreptitiously passing notes to classmates, and staring distractedly at the window. My attempts to generate discussions ended in sluggish question-and-answer exchanges that only confirmed my inability to fill the classroom void with the lively noise of engaged learners. No words were ever as painful as the silences permeating those first years of teaching.

Lacking the sanctuary of a seminar for new faculty or sympathetic colleagues to share my discomfort with, I inevitably read silence as failure. This sense of failure was all the more embarrassing because the subject of my classes was education itself. In retrospect, I understand the unrealistic images against which I measured myself, the alternative strategies that might have challenged apathetic undergraduates, and my own unwillingness to speak about the things that really mattered to me.

In those early days of teaching, I granted my unsuspecting students far too much power over my life in academia. Hurt and resentful because of their lack of interest, I failed to recognize that student silences are as likely to reflect their fears of the material as our communicative abilities. With time I became more conversant with these fears and the defensive mechanisms through which students try to keep them under control.

A turning point in my appreciation of silence occurred when I began to speak in class about being gay and how this affected my perspective on the state of American education. Coming out shifted some of my discomfort about teaching onto the students. The situation became less problematic for me, more disquieting for them. They began to question their prior assumptions about who can speak and who remains silent, about what teachers and students should know of each other's lives.

In the classroom our conversations became richer as I left behind the pose of objectivity. At the same time, I also began to welcome silences rather than to fear them. Here were opportunities to reflect on troubling questions, acknowledge unresolved issues, and experience unsettling emotions. Not wanting to foreclose these sometimes confusing, often provocative moments, I gave up the press to cover material in favor of the commitment to build a community of learners. Challenging the authority of the word to order and organize our time in class, I began to wonder about the way that communication occurs in and through silence, a process that was confirmed for me during my father's many illnesses.

Now there are often days when I arrive in my father's hospital or nursing home room with the *New York Times* in hand and it seems as if no words will be exchanged. With a brief nod for a greeting, he immediately points to the eagerly awaited reading matter. Then he proceeds to extract the business section, fold it into slender quarters—a skill that I admired as a young child and still have not mastered—and searches out the stock prices that he regularly tracks. Despite having no sight in one eye and very little in the other, he is able to identify the tiny abbreviations more successfully than any of his guests. I retire to a side chair by his bed and try to read or just sit quietly.

Ironically, my brother, who has long benefited from my father's investment advice and whose stocks my father was following but no longer trading, has little patience for this apparent indifference. Irritated, he tells me that he will quickly terminate his visit if my father continues to read. In contrast, I understand that my father is free to fill the time of my stay, never more than an hour, in whatever way he chooses. I make no claims on his attention. I am lending him my life for this brief bit of the week. Experience also teaches me that if I wait him out—five, ten, or twenty minutes, depending on the day—he will eventually look up and engage in a short conversation, with his voice when it still remained or with pad and paper when it was completely gone. Then, just as suddenly, he will return to the newspaper or drift off and I will continue to sit silently. I am satisfied simply to be in his presence and to appreciate his continuing interest in something other than his own health, which he is preoccupied with for most of his waking hours. I do not expect chatter or meaningful exchanges but am confident that all our time together matters deeply to both of us and happy for him to do with it as he wishes.

There are other days when, seriously depressed or raging with anger, my father says little or nothing. Then the silence is filled with a different set of emotions. The sullen withdrawal bespeaks despair. The silent rage is wielded like a sword to stab anyone he sees as responsible for his imprisonment within a body and institutions that he cannot control. Trying to break through such silence is often a thankless task, so mostly I choose to quietly observe. I am saddened by what I see yet hopeful that my father might eventually be made more comfortable. Working with children and caring for people with HIV/ AIDS makes clear that at times all we can do is bear witness to another's life. I can only offer my presence and now these pages as testimony to what occurs in those rooms.

I know that silence makes many people uncomfortable. Enmeshed in a culture that values verbal communication, it is often difficult for us to imagine different ways of being with and relating to others. Some of my graduate students are upset by a forty-five-minute videotape of a woman bathing her sister's baby in an Ivory Coast village. During this highly ritualized, twice-a-day practice, no words are spoken, nor are there any of the verbalizations deemed by our culture to be a "normal" part of infant-adult interactions. Instead we see rigorous physical caring in a hot, dusty, and severe environment. Similarly, viewing a film of a preschool in Japan, where teacher-student contacts are formal and spare, raises questions for my students about the role of adults in promoting language development. In Japan, instruction is delivered to relatively large groups of young children, and there is little opportunity for expressive language. Traditional culture rewards adults who are able to intuit the needs of others rather than articulate their own feelings. Teachers see intelligence reflected in a child's ability to fit into the group. Problematic children are those who stand out for any reason, who make their individual voices heard. The homogeneous societies of Japan and Africa place an ultimate value on membership in the collective, on empathy and action. In contrast, our heterogeneous society values the isolated individual, separation from others, and talk.

How do we come to read silence? How do we learn to remain still? My brother's own daughter describes one way this may happen. She and I are on one of those long Thanksgiving Day walks that can only occur if others are cooking and we are allowed to prepare for the indulgences to follow. Since my brother has lived most of his adult life in the Far East and I have really only known my niece through brief summer visits, she properly assumes that I am not in possession of the details of her family history.

I don't remember exactly what we talk about on the brief stretch of road leading down to the ocean. But I do recall that as we step onto the wintry beach, Anne, bundled against the cold Atlantic winds of late November, tells me how her parents first met.

"And how did you meet Bob?" she finally asks me. As I share this part of my own history, we laugh at the similarities. Like her parents, we were introduced by a mutual friend at a party. Similarly, we were too preoccupied with other people and projects to be immediately interested in one another.

On leaving the beach, our conversation takes an unexpected turn.

"You know when I realized you were gay, Uncle Jonathan?" Anne asks. I am unnerved, my stomach is unsettled even as my intellect is sparked. In truth, I'm not sure I want to know, but am unwilling to reject an offering that is so gently and hopefully proffered.

Ironically, Anne's knowing comes through a denial. It is an ordinary dinner table conversation that reveals an exceptional fact. Anne is nine or ten and has no memory of the prior topic but is clear about the moment when her mother turned to her father, saying, "Don't you think it's time we tell Anne about Jonathan?" My brother's response is crisp and declarative, paternal and paternalistic: "Absolutely not."

Unwittingly, his negative reply reveals everything he wished to keep hidden. My brother's denial is the exact moment Anne understands that I am gay. Now she understands the visit to our house several years before in a new way: the domestic routines that she participated in—the shopping, cooking and cleaning-up, the bedroom and double bed, the rituals of rainy-day card games, and trips to the summer beach that filled the sunny days. Bob was an elementary school teacher before becoming a photographer and had all the instincts to make such a potentially awkward family visit relaxing and fun. Although he taught slightly older children, sixth, seventh, and eighth graders, his sense of humor, so right for early adolescents, is appreciated by everyone.

None of the meaning of the events that Anne had participated in does she discuss with her mother; there are no difficult questions nor fumbled replies. Since she lives in a culture where sex is a private matter, and public displays of affection in bad taste, this is not surprising. Now, however, her mother's question functions as a statement. There is indeed *something* to tell. My brother's response affirms the need to hide that something, that family scandal.

For my part, I don't believe that the naming of sexual orientation, just like a declaration of marital status, reveals anything of a private, let alone scandalous, nature. What is private is how we choose to live out our identities. In this instance, the scandal is constituted by the silence of Anne's parents, not my sexual orientation. They behave as if they can protect her from experiences she has already had, from truths she already knows. It is their own passion for ignorance that provokes my niece's recognition.

As we draw close to home that Thanksgiving afternoon, I wonder aloud about the kind of knowing that led to Anne's untroubled dinner table insight. She tells me that she did not have negative attitudes about homosexuality. It is simply never discussed in Chinese culture. I believe it was the ongoing experience of hearing Bob and me spoken about, of seeing us do the things that people do as they live together, when the word "roommate" did not suffice to name the history, caring, and desire that bound our two lives together that laid the groundwork for Anne's understanding.

At first blush, remaining silent, holding a secret, may appear to be, indeed may feel like, an isolating act, something that we do alone. Yet in reality, secrets are always relational. When we keep ideas to ourselves, we often keep others at a distance. When we decide to share secrets, they connect us to particular people in a more intimate manner. Nor do secrets occur in a social vacuum. Their existence is predicated on a social system that defines private and public, shame and honor. Secrets structure the boundaries between self and other, between individual and society. Learning to keep secrets is part of healthy development, a sign that children understand how their particular social world works.

The poet J. D. McClatchy, in his essay "My Fountain Pen," describes the complexity and creative potential of the in-between spaces where queer people like me so often find ourselves. Aware of his homosexuality from a very early age, he learns, through writing, to make a distinction between hiding something, keeping a secret from others, and disguising it so as to make it difficult but not impossible for others to see.

> Long before I was given the fountain pen, of course, I had learned to hide things. Childhood's true polymorphous perversity, its constant source of both pleasure and power, is lying. But that pen helped me to discover

something better than the lie. Almost as soon as it was given to me, I learned to hide inside the pen. Or rather, the pen allowed me to learn the difference between *hiding* and *disguising* something—that is to say, making it difficult but not impossible to see. Even when I knew the difference, I couldn't always keep myself from confusing them.

McClatchy tells us that children are exquisitely attuned to the adult social world. My niece, for one, is an insightful reader of her parents' silence. McClatchy also tells us that early in life we develop identity by remaining silent. When we begin to withhold information or feelings from others, we begin to experience ourselves as separate from rather than merged with those around us. As interior dialogue develops, we are aware of ourselves in a new way. McClatchy knows himself as someone who struggles with the difference between hiding and disguising his feelings. I know myself as someone filled with desires for other boys and men. Anne knows herself as someone with a gay uncle. We are all busy on the inside coming to understand ourselves and quiet on the outside, allowing our self-knowledge to seep into the silences, to be read between the lines by those we trust to contain the secrets that help to shape our identities.

I do not remember any dramatic moments from my own childhood when an explicit silencing leads to a more articulated knowing about the world. What I do remember, however, is my ongoing interest in people who have differently organized lives from the one I know and my suspicions that there are meaningful worlds beyond our family that I might be connected to and implicated in. During the post–World War II years of conformity and celebration of the nuclear family, I value every opportunity to encounter people who live outside the mainstream. Developmentally appropriate curiosity, or protogay stirrings about nontraditional families?

The same year during which my father was mourning the death of his mother, my brother, then nine, receives special instruction from his third-grade teacher for a reading problem that would now probably be called dyslexia. Every Saturday morning I accompany him and my mother on the long subway ride from our solidly middle-class, Upper West Side neighborhood to the rundown brownstone on a Chelsea side street where she lives. Growing up in a large apartment building, I am fascinated by having to take several steps down from street level to enter her tiny garden flat and, once inside, to find all the cooking appliances built into the back wall, an arrangement that my mother knowingly refers to as a "Pullman" kitchen. And indeed, the Pullman cars in which we travel to visit relatives in distant cities are compact, contain everything within arm's reach, and seem completely modern in the same 1950s sort of way as this abbreviated kitchen. My mother's words summon up the glamour and excitement of those overnight train trips when we always wake up in just enough time to have breakfast in the dining car before arriving at our destination. The ethnic fabrics that are used to cover the well-worn furniture in the apartment and the handmade pottery from far-off countries that sits atop the tables and bookshelves expand the potential excitement that travel already held for me.

When I enter high school and spend time in Greenwich Village, I might label an apartment such as this "bohemian," signaling a much-romanticized way of life. But when I am six, this slightly shabby room, the bed disguised as a sofa during our daytime visits, the guitar resting against the wall, and the artifacts from other cultures, has an air of strange places, of a life that is unsettled and, for me, unsettling. Living as I do, surrounded by family—in addition to my parents and my brother we frequently have one or another of my father's unmarried sisters in residence for prolonged periods of time—I cannot make sense of an adult woman on her own. Besides, my aunts seem unmarried in a way that is different from the way that Marguerite Estrallow was unmarried. For there are no visible signs that I can now remember of family life in her environment, of the context of her singleness. Where does she come from and where does she really belong? Why does she live alone? Is she someone else's maiden aunt?

My own sixth-and-seventh-grade teacher is exotic in quite another way, but one that also suggests alternative, less middle-class,

ways of living. A pipe-smoking Harvard graduate with a serious Boston twang, always dressed in tweed sport jacket, graying hair pressed
back against his temples, Dick—in our progressive school first names
are de rigueur—is the scion of a large New England family. Generally
soft-spoken, when he loses his temper, he commands a booming voice
that sends darts into your stomach. But I mostly remember him as
a gentle man who loves to read aloud to us after lunch even when
we are too old for such an indulgence. Dick is given to mounting
semester-long theatrical productions that are the cause of many half-
hearted reminders about returning to the formal curriculum and to
taking us on weeklong study trips to Civil War battlefields, fading
Amish communities, and factories with strong labor unions.

We are aware that Dick is a renegade simply because he is a
Harvard-educated male teaching grade school. But we also sense
more. The only thing we know for sure is that Dick lives "uptown"
and that he is married to Gwen, an African American poet. At first
blush, an interracial marriage seems unremarkable in this educational
setting that welcomes refugees from McCarthy's purges and focuses on
issues of social justice in the curriculum. The theme of my brother's
1958 high school yearbook is "free expression," the Bill of Rights
proudly superimposed on its end pages. In reality, Black and white
students still live in different worlds. We learn about each other in
oblique ways. Race is framed abstractly as a civil-rights issue rather
than as a matter of individual social identity. An interracial marriage
is accepted but not discussed, a mystery that touches the heart of my
own particular unspoken anxieties about race and sexuality. In this
liberal enclave of the 1950s, we acquire the politically correct stance
toward many subjects but not necessarily the courage to pursue the
deeper personal questions and concerns they raise for us.

As we get older, Dick becomes our high school English teacher
and we also know that Gwen complains about the frequent play re-
hearsals that keep her husband in school so late. We do see her once
a year when she attends the opening night performance. Short and
heavy set, Gwen seems older than Dick, an inappropriate partner, I

think, for someone of his intense energy. In retrospect, I understand that while I am intrigued by their interracial marriage I also do not want to believe that Dick has any partner other than us, the students whom he obviously cares so much about. The existence of a spouse suggests that we might not always assume primacy in his life, that adults might manage deep emotional ties to several people at once.

Dick and Gwen's relationship poses a further complication for me because they do not appear to have any children in their immediate life. Although many of my classmates come from divorced homes—stepparents, weekend visits, if not joint custody, are an integral part of their world—the complete absence of children challenges my concept of family. Gwen and Dick's marriage hints that there might be alternative models that I haven't yet been exposed to. If their life does not focus on raising children, what brings them together? Why do they stay married?

I now realize that Bob and I may have served a similar function for Anne when she was growing up. Knowing us in even the limited way that occurred in her formative years might have enabled Anne to entertain new possibilities for imagining the future, perhaps even a queer future. Queer not necessarily in an explicitly sexual way, although there is always that, but queer in a socially nonconforming way, at least when viewed against the backdrop of the choices that her own parents had made.

There is no small irony in the fact that my appreciation of silence is in part what allows me to bear witness to my father's suffering in his last years. For while this appreciation is deeply embedded in my gay history—filled as it was with a curiosity about social differences of all kinds and the management of secrets—initially such an anathema to him, it is ultimately essential to tolerating his difficult times. Caring for my father expands my understanding of silence from a socially oppressive phenomenon to a medium through which complex interpersonal communications also transpire. This new awareness of how silence can function as communicative action does not replace but rather exists alongside my earlier understandings so powerfully encapsulated in the Silence = Death slogan of 1980s AIDS activists.

Finally, teaching about the tension between silence and voice, trying to make sense of the unspoken communications with my father, I look to queer theorist Eve Sedgwick for help. Prompted by a cancer diagnosis to reflect on her life, Sedgwick reads the classic Buddhist writings. Eschewing autobiography, the more traditional vehicle authors frequently use when facing death, she discovers in these texts a kind of pedagogical meditation in which the deathbed is continually produced as a privileged scene of teaching. Here too she finds the student and teacher roles are interchangeable. The caregiver receives far more than she is ever able to give. Means and ends are confounded. Death is a means to some further ends. Death is a problem to be solved with skillful means. We strive to live with the continual consciousness of death and to die as we have lived.

In *Touching Feeling* Sedgwick recognizes that a central role of the teacher is to point to the world, identifying a problem or experience worthy of the student's attention. She is not very sanguine, however, about the process entailed in such pointing. She is drawn to the space between language and experience, the object and its signifier, means and ends. In Buddhist writing, this pedagogical conundrum is referred to as "pointing at the moon." As Walter Hsieh comments in *A Treasury of Mahāyāna Sūtras*:

> Employing speech as a skillful means, the Buddha spoke many sutras, which should only be taken as "the finger that points to the moon," not the moon itself. The Buddha said, "I have not taught a single word during the forty-nine years of my Dharma preaching." The sutras often admonish us to rely on meaning rather than on mere words.... Readers should bear in mind that it is not the words themselves but the attachment to words that is dangerous.

Dangerous attachments. Words and texts can take on a life of their own, cut off from the experiences in which they are grounded. Lives like my father's can produce fewer and fewer texts and are lived at an increasing distance from those who love them. What exactly am I learning about silence at my father's bedside?

After many anxious and guilt-ridden conversations, my brother and I decide that we can no longer manage my father's care at his apartment. He will remain permanently in the nursing home where he has gone after suffering a broken hip in 2000. His response to our carefully worded presentation is oblique, "Well . . . I am pretty well adjusted here for the period that they would find acceptable. After all, they aren't going to get people with a twenty-year life expectancy. I am not rehabilitated yet."

I am taken aback, worried that he doesn't understand the permanent nature of the decision. When I reiterate that he will be moving to another floor and giving up his greatly prized single room, he indicates optimism as well as realism, "I may be dreaming," he writes, "but I keep feeling that maybe I will progress to better days."

A week later I am still pressing home the point, hoping for what? Accusations, regrets, resolutions, cathartic words? It's just after dinner. Because of my father's difficulties swallowing, meals can last an hour or more. And because he communicates only with pen and paper, these are quiet occasions. I am eager to leave and eager for reassurance. "Dad, you know, if there's anything you want to talk about, well, this might be a good time," I say. I hand him the yellow legal pad on which he slowly and carefully prints these words, "Of course there is a lot I could talk about. But most of it is too painful to even think about." Indeed, it's too painful to think about because it has already been thought. He is pointing to the moon; the pointing and the moon are both the same and distinct.

I am still for a long time. Then I tell him, "Well, if you ever feel like talking, I am strong enough to hear what you have to say." Of course, this bravado indicates the very opposite, my vulnerability rather than any strength. With a detached smile and a turn toward the television set, my father terminates our conversation. A master of words has spoken through his silence.

8

My Father, His Psychiatrists, and Me

> Every analysis, in a sense, is about the obstacles
> to memory: people come for psychoanalysis
> because the way they are remembering their
> lives has become too painful; the stories they
> are telling themselves have become too coercive
> and restrictive. In so far as they have a dominant
> story about who they are, they have a repetitive
> story. And repetition, for Freud, is forgetting in
> its most spellbinding form.
>
> ADAM PHILLIPS, *Flirtation*

Back when my father was eighty-seven, a time at which many bodies
break down beyond repair, and no longer a candidate for medical interventions available to younger, more vital men, he was patched together with the help of a feeding tube, hearing aids, a walker, diapers,
and the twelve medications that allowed him to get through each day.
Weakened and depressed by repeated illnesses, he has reason enough
to be angry. Nonetheless, his sudden outbursts have become so frequent and intimidating that I am increasingly reluctant to call or
visit, let alone speak with him about issues critical to his care. In more

reflective moments, my father counsels me not to be afraid and insists that I can ask him anything. These reassurances don't carry much weight with me these days.

Having lost control over his body, my father tries to assert his authority in other arenas. In the period between his first and second cancer surgeries, he redoubles his efforts to manage his personal finances. He is unable to remember facts and figures as he once did or to do the complicated mental math that my entire family had always been in awe of. He urges me to use the new hand-held calculator that sits on his desk but does not resort to it himself. Treating me like an incompetent employee who does not devote sufficient time to the job, he showers me with bitter harangues about my failure to keep him informed of his income and expenses. But no amount of information can satisfy him now because he retains little and because he is no longer amenable to rational argument.

After one particularly acrimonious dispute has died down, I comment on his determination to stay on top of things. Alluding to our argument, my father responds with a self-satisfied laugh, "Yeah, I knew you were coming so I marshaled my energy." I laugh along with him and admit that I felt ambushed, totally unprepared for his sudden attack. In truth, I am made uneasy by my father's rapid shifts of mood and his canny insights. His laughter sounds unnatural, the lingering residue of an earlier hospital psychosis. A masklike persona hides an incomprehensible personality shift.

At the same time, I can't help but wonder when I became the enemy, an intruder whom my father prepares to do battle with. Was it the day I took my parents to the lawyer who pointed out the inadequacies of their carefully drawn but long-outdated plans for their final years? Was it the day when, because he was suffering from the effects of severe dehydration, my mother and I coerced him to go to the hospital against his will? Or was it some far more distant event, even the sum of our history together, that makes me both a loved and a provocative presence to him? My father's ambivalence toward me, the caregiver who has assumed responsibility for financial and medical decision making, is never hidden, always on display.

Once my father takes aim, I am an easy mark for his rage. With inadequate internal defenses, I soak up his anger and anxiety like a dry sponge. When he is in the hospital, I wake up in the middle of the night worrying if he is asleep or needs help getting to the bathroom. It is an unsettling feeling as I imagine myself in his room but am unable to protect him from discomfort, and I can't fall back to sleep. We have made a mess of the boundaries that might have enabled us to maintain a healthier degree of sovereignty in our own psychic domains.

I know that my father's anger is a sign of life, a vital assertion of his presence in the world. He will not be ignored. He rails against the gap between the image he once projected—in charge, self-sufficient, proudly independent—and the reality of who he has become, someone reliant on others to satisfy the most basic needs, from eating and drinking to getting out of bed and dressing in the morning. But he rails against more than the loss of physical mobility. According to the Rousseauean ideal, a truly free person "wants only what he can get, and does only what pleases him." Happiness is possible only when our powers and desires are in accord. My father is a slave caught between his desires and his inability to fulfill them. Rousseau's maxim aside, contemporary psychologists suggest that the story of human development may be understood as the growing recognition of this tension, of the space between self and other, as well as our growing skill at securing what we want. In old age, my father is painfully aware of the gap between his wants and his ability to fend for himself. He is a good learner but not a fast learner and is slow to adapt to these changed circumstances.

My social worker friends tell me that the elderly want to talk about the past. They say that constructing a coherent life narrative is a therapeutic process through which my parents will be able to place events and people in meaningful relationship to each other. Revising their story to incorporate recent illnesses will help them to attain control over uncontrollable events, to understand the new catastrophes in terms of familiar themes. Through such talk they may give shape and finality to their losses. At a time when visits to professionals dominate daily life, my parents can assert expertise with the authoritative telling of their lives.

Although such a life-review process is not one in which they normally engage with me, I do see it in action on the cold, rainy winter day that a nurse comes to evaluate my parents for enrollment in Medicaid. They have fiercely fought the Medicaid designation but have finally resigned themselves and know that the interview is critical to remaining in their own apartment. I arrive late, tied up in city traffic, and harassed, but the nurse arrives even later and more harassed. I presume that the nurse will want to hear directly from my parents so that she can assess their emotional and cognitive impairments as well as their physical disabilities. I understand my job as facilitative and plan to stay in the background as much as possible. At the same time I am eager to monitor my parents' storytelling so that the medical details, diagnoses, and limitations of their functioning insure their eligibility for Medicaid.

I need not have worried. My father does a full and complete job of recounting the last years. He subtly and coolly displays his intellect and connectedness to the world. Before my arrival he has even located the 1989 MRI documenting his spinal stenosis, the disease that has made his walking so precarious, which the nurse will look at gravely but respectfully return to him for safekeeping. He will also pull items from a notebook overflowing with health updates, information about stocks and investment options, and news clippings about research on the radiation scarring that has left his throat burned and filled with mucus. The experienced nurse quickly adjusts to my father's speech, which is very slow and barely audible. Surprisingly he doesn't mind when I add dates or resequence events. At times like this, after the battle about applying for Medicaid has long passed, we can work like a team. He knows that Medicaid assistance is the only way to pay for his fifteen-hundred-dollar-a-month drug bills and to secure partial reimbursement for the around-the-clock health aides that keep him out of a nursing home.

My mother's performance is more mixed. She overstates some aspects of her physical condition and underestimates others. She can recite the days of the week but does not know the date, can subtract seven from one hundred continuing back to fifty-one but cannot repeat a simple series of numbers. My mother is skillful at hiding her cognitive deficits, the result of many small strokes, and I am relieved when the nurse recognizes them. Because we have started so late and the interview moves so slowly I cannot stay until the end. As I prepare to leave I catch a final glimpse of my father lying on his bed, waiting for the nurse to examine the feeding tube that he now needs to assure that sufficient liquids and nourishment reach his system.

On the bus ride to work, I am unexpectedly swamped with emotions, proud of how well my parents have told their story and weighed down by how much time and energy is required to keep their household afloat. The nurse makes good, practical suggestions: My father should be on liquid medications, which will be easier to swallow. But who will contact three different doctors to arrange such a change? My mother should go out for twenty minutes every day. But who will fight that battle? Certainly not the single caregiver who must supervise my father and remain on good terms with my mother.

On the day of the nurse's visit the storytelling seems to have been cathartic, if exhausting, for everyone. But on so many other occasions my father disregards my well-intentioned, if misguided, invitations to revisit the past. From his perspective, he knows only that something has gone terribly wrong. He will not settle until it is fixed. Like an infant's primary caregiver, I am the recipient of powerfully ambivalent emotions evoked by his new dependence. He does not offer any philosophic renderings of a life well spent. I am loved and feared, respected and hated, seduced and abandoned when I don't do his bidding. As the chosen target of his resentments, I am also the one who enables him to keep his story alive. For as long as my father insists and refuses, plots against me and strategizes to undermine my new powers, his drama continues. I understand the many small crises, the excitements, as self-induced incitements to stay the final curtain from falling.

Unfortunately, all this understanding cannot quell my sense of inadequacy, of not being up to providing the care that my father needs. As he rages over a misplaced doctor's bill, bank statement, or phone number, I envision him gasping for one last breath before succumbing to a heart attack provoked by my clumsy and inept response to his diatribe. Aspirations of revenge punctuate my thoughts. I imagine his funeral, the few remaining friends and family, and the kind things that others will say. I am silent and experience only a tremendous sense of relief.

No matter what the origins of his anger, or how it functions to insure his survival, I cannot tolerate the situation any longer. In the hope that some modern pharmaceutical miracle might ease his discomfort and enable me to care for him and my mother, I persuade my father to consult with a psychopharmacologist. We no longer have the luxury of the time required for the more traditional talking cures.

My determination to make things better for all of us, however, is quickly deflated as I approach the building where we are to meet with the doctor that autumn afternoon. From across Madison Avenue I see my father, assisted by Marlene, his health aide, just emerging from a taxi. My mother, impelled forward by her own anxiety, is already at the entrance of the building. My father, who refuses to use a wheelchair in public, leans into his walker. Marlene shadows him from behind to prevent a backward fall. His heavy winter overcoat, buttoned high around the neck against the cold November day, conceals his shrunken frame and emaciated body. He moves slowly and distractedly toward the sidewalk. I watch from a safe distance as he tackles the curb. I imagine Marlene telling him, in her kindly yet authoritative Jamaican accent, "Lift your foot, Mr. Silin. Lift your foot now." It is as if she must coordinate his physical movements by sending to various parts of the body messages that are usually sent from the inside, by the brain.

In contrast to his body, which works in slow motion, every movement an effort of extreme will, my father's mind functions at high speed. Often it seems that too many communications are being sent at once, causing them to become confused and misrouted, content and emotion thrown together pell-mell. After all, isn't that why we are about to assemble in the doctor's office? Yet, seeing my father from a distance, as others must see him, a weak and fragile old man, I have second thoughts. Who is really to benefit from this visit? Wouldn't a more stoic attitude on my part be less taxing on all of us?

As the light changes for a second time, I take a deep breath and hurry across the street. Leaving aside hesitations, I join my father, careful to announce myself in a voice loud enough so that he can hear me but not so intrusively as to startle him. He stops, looks up, and smiles at me warmly.

Although the building is old and probably once contained spacious office suites and apartments, it has been modernized in a haphazard way. Everything is cramped and small. The doctor's waiting room is no more than a hallway with chairs strung out in a line against one wall, and there is no receptionist to greet us. A far cry from the expansive and well-staffed waiting rooms of my youth, here it is hard for the four of us to maneuver in these close quarters—to hang up coats and hats and to find space for the walker, my overstuffed backpack, and the all-important brown paper bag filled with my father's pills.

The office itself, dominated by a cluttered desk piled high with manila folders and drug samples, requires that I bring in additional seats from the waiting room to accommodate us. Once we are settled inside and after my opening explanation of our visit, Dr. R turns to my father. In a controlled voice, the anger seething just beneath the surface, my father delivers a ten-minute indictment of all those involved in his care. Everyone—family, friends, and professionals—has failed to respond adequately to his physical needs and to appreciate the depths of his suffering. His words are direct, his thoughts well organized, and his focus clear.

My mother and I are each allotted a brief time to recount our recent experiences with my father. But Dr. R is no family therapist and takes little interest in our stories. He attends only to the identified patient. As we talk, Dr. R dumps out the contents of the brown bag on to the desk and copies down the names and dosages of my father's medications. Noting the antidepressant drugs, he asks my father if he has been to a psychiatrist before. My father answers by talking about Dr. M, a well-known psychoanalyst whom he saw regularly during the 1950s. Dr. R pursues a line of questioning—did my father sit or lie down during the sessions? Did he go three or five times a week?—designed to reveal if my father was in a classical analysis. No, my father insists, he always sat up and could not possibly afford five sessions a week. He chuckles to himself as he reports that Dr. M found his case so interesting that he often allowed him to pay whatever he could. From time to time, he even asked my father's advice about the stock market. My father reserves for himself a special place in Dr. M's practice and refuses standard categories. When Dr. R makes explicit his own assumption that my father was in therapy for depression, my father reacts quickly and sharply. "No," he asserts, "I was not depressed, although I didn't feel great. I went to Dr. M because I was dissatisfied with my life. Because I thought I could do better."

I am stunned by this carefully considered formulation. During the years of my own psychotherapy, I had developed an understanding of my father as a deeply depressed person, which I had never questioned before. Nor can I reconstruct exactly how this understanding came about. Perhaps it was more a reflection of my own situation than my lived experience of his frequent moodiness, occasional tears, and demanding ways. In contrast to my therapeutic attempts to stave off existential despair and emotional paralysis, my father suggests something quite different about himself—a drive to improve his situation.

My father was ambitious as well as dissatisfied, determined as well as unhappy.

At this moment in Dr. R's office, just a few streets north but many decades removed from Dr. M's practice, my father displays his continuing ability to rise to the occasion, to show himself to best advantage. He still has resources to draw on, accounts that have not been completely emptied. Despite all his infirmities, my father does not present himself as a victim but rather as someone who wants to live up to his potential. He is ready to accept professional help in a way that preserves his pride and emphasizes his sense of agency. His story of Dr. M is as much about the present as about the past.

I will never know the truth of my father's clinical diagnosis, although I did come to know Dr. M, who acted as a kind of family therapist long before that discipline was invented. He is part of my history as well as my father's, and I remember our first encounter vividly.

I am a shy, anxious child, a bed wetter who, according to my mother's oft-repeated words, lacks self-confidence. My first visit to Dr. M is the emotional equivalent of a general checkup. His office, located on the ground floor of narrow brownstone, consists of a waiting room in the front and a large office in the rear of the building. These rooms do not open directly onto each other but are connected by a narrow passageway with doors at either end, so that privacy is assured. In these days before white noise machines and Muzak, it is the architecture itself that assures privacy. I don't recall the content of our conversations or of any play that I might have engaged in. But I do remember that near the end of this session, I admire a tiny balsa wood model, no more than two or three inches long, of an old sailing ship replete with linen sails and painted designs on the side. I am fascinated by this model and, before I leave, Dr. M asks me if I would like to have it. I hold the boat carefully in my hands as I rejoin my mother in the waiting room. Deeply satisfied with my gift and our visit, I do not mind at all when she leaves me alone in the waiting room to

have a private conversation with Dr. M. Later, on the street, she pro-
nounces me perfectly healthy and happy. Shortly after, the bed-
wetting stops.

My second meeting with Dr. M is as deeply unsettling as the first
is satisfying. I have just dropped out of college, am living at home
again, and have become ensconced in an affair with a married man
more than twice my age. I know I am homosexual by age thirteen but
begin to live out my gayness only when I start college. There I em-
brace my homosexuality with such fervor that there is little energy left
for anything else. My erotic and affective life are all that matter. Despite the best efforts of a well-meaning college psychiatrist, academic
pursuits quickly fall by the wayside. Paralyzed by two unsuccessful relationships, I eventually leave school, but not before the psychiatrist
can make one final pronouncement about my prospects. "On aver-
age," he cautions in his most concerned tone of voice, "homosexual
liaisons don't last more than a few weeks or, at best, several months.
Only in the rarest cases do they last two years, the outer limit of same-
sex relationships." After summarizing these latest research findings on
homosexuality, he telegraphs two seemingly contradictory messages
in the Morse code of therapeutic jargon: I have willfully chosen this
road to ongoing suffering and disappointment; I am only going
through a difficult stage, a developmentally appropriate adolescent
identity crisis. Whether I am simply the victim of development gone
awry or a free agent who is making a perverse choice, however, the
doctor reassures me that the course on which I have set out can be
reversed with proper professional help. "Help," fortunately, that I do
not find.

At the same moment that I am learning my fate in one office of
the new 1960s modern health services building that we affectionately
refer to as the "Magic Mountain," a fellow classmate, the writer An-
drew Holleran, is receiving similar instruction just next door. In a
1993 interview he describes seeking help because he suspects that he
might be homosexual. Although Holleran finds a sympathetic ear at
his initial interview, the psychiatrist to whom he is referred, and to

whom he guiltily reports his failure to make sexual overtures to the woman he is dating at a nearby woman's college, resorts to more curmudgeonly if direct advice, "Well, next time, go kiss her!" No need to cite the latest research, to become entangled in needless self-doubt, or to return for future sessions.

Recently, I learned that after years of marriage, children, and the heterosexual life, my own Magic Mountain doctor has finally come out. He is living happily with a man who is considerably younger than he is. Perhaps he spent too long seeking proper help, as did Dr. Ralph Roughton, the prominent psychoanalyst profiled in the *New York Times* who came out at age sixty-three after two long analyses in which he tried to become straight. While I recognize that most people may go through some struggle in coming to terms with their sexuality, I cannot help but feel bitter irony when Dr. Roughton's 1998 act is described by his peers as courageous. My own admiration is reserved for the gay activists of 1973 who successfully lobbied the American Psychiatric Association to remove homosexuality from its list of mental disorders and for the first openly gay doctors who entered psychoanalytic training in the early 1990s.

But back in 1963, despite my determined efforts to find romantic happiness, I am not feeling very courageous or admirable myself. Upset by my extreme mood swings that alternated with long periods of inertia, my parents send me to see Dr. M again. I agree to go because of my favorable memories. Notwithstanding the college psychiatrist's assessment of my prospects for future happiness, I had become very attached to him and do not want to begin therapy with someone totally unknown. Dr. M is already part of my world and seems an obvious choice.

In the end, however, Dr. M proves too much a part of that world. Although my father's analysis concluded before I was an adolescent, his work with Dr. M did not enable him to treat me with equanimity. The heat of our relationship reflects the intensity of our mutual attachment. My father acts as an emotional lightning rod, attracting the electricity that breaks through the storm clouds almost always hanging in the air. The resulting sparks set off countless brushfires that require all my mother's mediating skills to keep them from spreading out of control.

Not shy about my gayness, at least in the therapeutic setting, I am soon telling Dr. M about my feelings for other men and the pleasures I find in their arms. He listens carefully and thoughtfully. At first he seems to be the patient, nonjudgmental father I long for. Unfortunately, he soon reveals himself to be the father I know so well, the father with confused boundaries and overwrought identifications. He tells me that my father loved to hold me as a baby, that I was a particularly warm and responsive infant, a source of physical and emotional sustenance for him. How am I, a young gay man who has experienced short crushes on peers but already fallen deeply in love with two older men, one a father of a young child himself, to make sense of Dr. M's confidence? Is he telling me that he knows from my early life that I have the makings of a responsive partner, someone capable of providing great satisfactions to another man? Is he telling me that my father is the source of my erotic longings and the later desire to reexperience early pleasures?

In part, I know Dr. M speaks the truth about my relationship with my father. After all, I have my own deep reservoir of bodily memories —riding atop my father's shoulders to watch soldiers coming home from World War II, sitting on his lap as he ate dinner long after we children had finished, lying in bed with him at night when I couldn't sleep. Nonetheless, I am unready to hear Dr. M's report from the past. News of my father's sensuality contaminates my blossoming sexuality. Filled with my own complex and ambivalent emotions, I do not want to hear about my father's desires and my role in their fulfillment. I certainly do not want to think of my father's connection to me as erotically charged, nor am I experienced enough to understand that the sensual enjoyment he received in holding me might be distinct from a specifically sexual one.

Now I imagine that my father, against the male stereotype of the 1940s, may have permitted himself some of the same pleasures that women report who breastfeed their children and are otherwise physically bonded with them. Indeed, it is hard to imagine otherwise. I recall the discomfort of my undergraduate students, especially the males, when I suggest the sensuous pleasures, tinged with incestuous and potentially homoerotically charged desires, that might be enjoyed by parent and young child. Were my own feelings of discomfort any different from those of my students? It is easier for them, I imagine, to deny these possibilities or to entertain them as theoretically interesting ideas in a classroom than it was for me, trapped as I was in a therapist's office with someone who could validate the specificity of my father's feelings. Experiencing great difficulty breaking away from my parents, I did not need to be reminded of the ties that bound me to them. Dr. M insisted on speaking the language of attachment and connection while I tried to speak the language of separation and divorce. How could I ever trust him to keep my own confidences when he willingly revealed my father's?

Dr. M made what I still consider to be a daring therapeutic move by revealing my father's sensuous attachment to me. It is also one that failed, if judged only by my immediate decision not to return for further help. In the succeeding years, however, I managed to transform the discomfort caused by Dr. M's maneuver into a guiding set of questions that I continue to explore in my work as an early childhood educator: What kind of knowledge can children tolerate about their teachers, teachers about their students, children about their parents? How does this tolerance change over time? I am drawn to teach what is most personally difficult for me. In the end, I believe that good teachers, like effective researchers, use the classroom to explore that which confounds and troubles them. How boring it would be to do otherwise.

Through most of my adult life, I maintain a carefully modulated distance from my parents. This seems the best way to protect myself from their emotional intrusiveness and the porous boundaries that make separation so difficult. Like many gay people, this means that I live in a glass closet for a very long time. My parents and I simply agree not to acknowledge that I am gay. Then in the mid-1970s, with my increasing political activity, I decide to shatter this closet with an official announcement about my sexual orientation.

The dining room—in which our later conversations about their care and my father's tirades about his loss of control will take place —is thick with emotion. There are no raised voices, however, or obvious shock expressed by my parents. This interview is about transforming unarticulated into articulated knowing. My parents are far from stupid. They know their children well. Besides, I am too old, and too much the black sheep, for them to think that being gay is a temporary stage in my life. For my parents, the moment seems to be about sadness and loss. My father expresses fears for my safety, for the potential prejudice that I may experience. Perhaps he is remembering the anti-Semitism he endured in his own childhood.

My mother's most potent protest is to decry the fact that I will not have children. Although I am not sure if they feel bereft for me or for themselves, this disappointment is understandable. After all, they have built their own lives around their children. At that moment, my parents cannot seem to separate what they know about me as an individual from the way that gay people are so often characterized—as selfish and self-absorbed because of the absence of children in their lives. I remind my parents of my work as a nursery school teacher. At best, they see this vocation as an inadequate substitute for raising children of one's own. They counter with embarrassing comments about the genes that will be lost if I decide not to reproduce. I am left speechless by their hubris, and the conversation ends.

In retrospect what strikes me about this conversation is the combination of fear and sorrow that drives my parents' response. These are not new themes, and perhaps it is only the baldness with which they are stated that takes me aback. After all, protectiveness, the worry that I am somehow vulnerable and will be the target of physical or emotional harm, preoccupied my parents throughout my childhood. The grief that I will not reproduce is an iteration of the elitism that has characterized their approach to my upbringing from the beginning. However my parents understand their family's special talents, they are now endangered because there may be no grandchildren, at least from this son. They are caught up in a set of narrow, dare I say narcissistic, ideas about how one generation lives through and influences another. In the end, there are no questions about intimacy, love, and the gay world in which I live: No curiosity about what being gay means to me, only statements about what it means to them.

It is at about this time, 1978, that I go to see Dr. M for the last time. In 1963 he had opened a door just wide enough for me to peer into a space where my father and my infant self could be seen in mutual rapture. Back then actually entering such a room felt intolerably threatening. Only fourteen years later do I feel secure enough to visit Dr. M, now ostensibly for professional advice.

We meet at Dr. M's office in the highly respected therapeutic nursery school that he helped to found. Having spent ten years teaching young children, I want to refocus my career, and Dr. M, a colleague of Anna Freud, seems an appropriate person with whom to discuss possible study at her clinic in London. In retrospect, the answer to my specific question—how will my application as an openly gay man be received?—is obvious. Even then, nearly ten years after Stonewall, my professional pride is loath to accept exclusion from what my educator colleagues judge to be the seat of therapeutic knowledge. My very presence in Dr. M's office is paradoxical. I am eager to proclaim my mental health and seek approval from someone whose earlier remarks, at best, were a clinical error in judgment and, at worst, left me deeply disturbed.

My question makes the usually confident Dr. M uncomfortable. Perhaps it is that I have forced him to articulate the popular clichés and biases that have dominated the psychoanalytic world until recently and announce a professional judgment on my life that causes him difficulty. I would like to think that Dr. M had not succumbed to the worst excesses of analytic thought and had approved of the 1973 American Psychological Association decision to excise homosexuality from its official list of psychiatric disorders.

I cannot know where Dr. M himself stands on the subject of homosexuality. He doesn't say, and the silence following my question is long and palpable. When he does respond, his words are smooth and skillfully crafted: "I think you might be more comfortable elsewhere. There are many places to train that would be more receptive to your application"—but the emotions are less polished and more jagged. Now it is I who have opened the door and Dr. M who has firmly closed it. I have the answer to my question as well as his pronouncement on my suitability to serve among the analytic elite. I leave feeling strangely content.

Ironically, when I turn to one of the few openly gay psychiatrists of that era to continue the conversation cut short in Dr. M's office, I once again encounter my father. In our very first session, this psychiatrist confides the he grew up in the same small city in western Pennsylvania as my father and remembers him well. He proceeds to ask after my father's five siblings by name, cannily characterizing each one with the briefest comments. I find no comfort in this familiarity, with this blurred, dare I say contaminated, fault line. Much to the doctor's consternation, I terminate the relationship immediately after solving my professional quandaries.

During these and succeeding years Bob and I attend the requisite family functions at the same time as I manage to sustain a necessary emotional space between my parents and myself. Then, with their first hospitalizations in the mid-1990s, it is no longer possible to do this. Perhaps the vulnerable body is what puts the emotional issues in perspective. Shockingly at first, all modesty falls by the wayside as well. Detailed reports about food consumed and left untouched on the tray, body fluids collected and resisting collection, weight gained and lost, preoccupy us all. I know more than I want to know about their bodily functions, just as I am forced to learn my way around their Byzantine financial arrangements. I struggle to master the multiple bank accounts, insurance polices, and safety deposit boxes that make it all but impossible to grasp the real limits of their resources. Attempting to keep track of the household expenses, I discover the daily economies my mother makes to secret away small amounts of money —the refusal to buy in quantity for fear they will not live to use the products, the stacks of outdated newspaper coupons promising fifty cents off three cans of soup, the down-to-the-penny reports she extracts from whoever does the shopping. All this laying bare of the practical arrangements by which they stitch together their lives is poignant and painful. I do what is required, knowing that, in the interest of preserving a modicum of my parents' dignity, some mysteries are better preserved than unearthed. Whether it is simply the passage of time, the years of therapy, or learning to write through my experience, none of my newly acquired insights is as threatening as the revelation offered by Dr. M so long ago.

Knowing much about the dailyness of my parents' lives leads me to make new comparisons. I want to replicate their best qualities and rewrite their less endearing traits. Bob teases me when I worry about the future at the expense of enjoying the present, "You're getting more like your father every day." He wants to continue with our plan to rent a house in the south of France from a writer friend even though I have suddenly lost all my consulting contracts and will come back to no work. He is used to living on the financial edge; the house is a bargain, a dream fulfilled. "How can we not go?" he asks. When I am reluctant to see other people, to give up a weekend of work and privacy to enjoy time at the beach with friends, Bob chides, "Be careful, or otherwise you will end up a recluse like your mother." I give in to his more social nature and am happy for the decision. Bob sees my parents in me and he is mostly right. I am more readily fooled by the huge discrepancies in our outward life circumstances and it isn't easy for me or for them to see the underlying patterns of behavior that connect us.

Connecting patterns. Oddly enough, my most recent therapist, Dr. C, an openly gay man, inherited the office at the therapeutic nursery school where Dr. M and I talked in 1978. This link between Dr. C and Dr. M is reinforced when Dr. C shares with me a recent dream he has had about the office. Here Dr. C displays some of his own therapeutic daring, a willingness to use himself to provoke my own reflection. I don't know if Dr. C actually met or worked with Dr. M. It is sufficiently complicated for me to know that Dr. C has sat where Dr. M once sat, the same place that decades earlier Dr. M may have thought about my father, his infant son, and even my grandfather. For just as Dr. C has listened to my family saga, and helped me to edit and reimagine my stories, so must Dr. M have heard my father out. Dr. M was undoubtedly the recipient of emotions intended for, and shaped by, my father's relationship with his father, Nathan Silin, for whom I was named. Queer genealogies.

We are two generations of men, my father and I, who share not only an abiding interest in children but also therapists with similar commitments. And my grandfather? While he was of Freud's generation, with no therapeutic canon or army of therapists to consult quite yet, I have increasingly wondered about the legacy that he bequeathed to my father and through him to me. Nathan, who died in 1940, four years before my birth, has always been portrayed as a distant if benevolent patriarch whose behavior was beyond reproach. He was the man of learning who earned his passage to America by traveling across Russia taking inventory of the Catholic churches in the four different languages that he spoke and wrote. Once here, he was the itinerant peddler turned successful merchant who fathered six children, all of whom attended college. Active in the local Jewish community, Nathan was an ideal citizen, husband, and father, someone who took the time to write regularly to each of his children while they were away at school. Little wonder that my own father has difficulty living up to these images and that he cannot permit himself to be a success. Tyrannized by his ideals, he keeps a hypervigilant watch on his own behavior and on that of the ones he loves. This patrimony, which excludes all reference to pleasure and desire, is one that I resist but that I all too easily succumb to. It is the narrow patrimony of work and self-sacrifice that Bob understands so well when he alerts me to the decisions that will narrow my social landscape and only reinforce my risk-averse nature.

I have not seen Dr. M since 1978. Occasionally I hear his name mentioned in professional circles, and from time to time my father wistfully wonders if he is still alive and seeing patients. As in my childhood, my father refers to Dr. M by his first name, Theodore, bestowing a kind of respectful intimacy on their relationship and on his presence as a shadow member of our family. I check the phone book and find that Dr. M's number is still listed. I imagine orchestrating a final interview that would satisfy my father's curiosity and my own. Ambivalence paralyzes these good intentions.

If Dr. M is part of my history, then Dr. R, the psychopharmacologist I persuade my ailing father to see, is an important part of the present. At the time of our initial interview, he adds a mood stabilizer to my father's already extensive mental health diet, which, he hopes, will prevent the sudden angry outbursts. He promises to monitor the results and regulate the dosage in bimonthly meetings with my father.

Six months later, my father is more even-tempered with me but continues cruelly to berate others around him. At a moment when my feelings of responsibility for my father's care outweigh my desire to allow him as much privacy as possible, I call Dr. R. His tone is one of impatience, and I imagine that he is probably between patients. He listens to my concerns about my father's continued outbursts but quickly moves to put them in biographical perspective. He leads me to acknowledge that they are not totally new to my father's personality. Dr. R chides, "We can't work miracles, you know." He makes me feel foolish, not a good clinical move, but then I am not the patient, only an intrusive caregiver. I am being too demanding again, I tell myself, but clearly my father's son.

My father is demanding of others but no less critical of himself. While he can forgive others, he has never learned to forgive himself. I wonder if he has himself ever been forgiven? He says he went to see Dr. M because he was not living up to his potential. His disappointments are legion, and I can't help but wonder if I am counted among them.

• • •

Several weeks after the initial visit to Dr. R, my father's eldest sister dies at the age of ninety-two. Notified by the nursing home that she is in her last hours, he manages, with the help of Marlene, his health aide, to arrive at her beside seconds before she expires. Later that same day he insists on going to the funeral home to make arrangements for the burial. Exhausted, he has done everything that he possibly can. For the rest, it is up to me to shoulder a full load of filial responsibilities. As a favorite nephew, I am also a stand-in child of my aunt, who might best be described, in the language of her time, as childless rather than with the more positive, contemporary phrase "child-free." Her husband had been dead for many years.

The day of the funeral is long and trying for everyone. At the cemetery it is cold and blustery, and Marlene can't push my father's wheelchair over the astroturf mats that hide the irregular mounds of freshly shoveled earth. Bob and I must lift the wheelchair with my father in it and carry him close to the graveside. The dozen family members and friends, almost all well over eighty themselves, are huddled together for warmth. Just as the rabbi is about to start the services, my father announces that he wants to look in the coffin. Seeking more than confirmation of his sister's death or an emotional farewell, my father wishes to assure himself that it is indeed her body and not someone else's being placed in the grave. He trusts no one, especially the undertaker.

My father's request unnerves the cemetery employees. They confide in hushed tones that it might upset other family members to see the body. My father is insistent, and my attempts to dissuade him useless. Finally, realizing the passion and compulsion behind my father's demand, I tell the cemetery people that there will be no funeral unless they do his bidding. Reluctantly, they lift the cover, and my father strains forward to satisfy his desire. Suddenly I see that, if he leans farther forward, he will fall out of his chair and into the grave. I quickly step in front of the two people next to me and place my hands on his shoulders to restrain him. Fortunately, he needs only a brief look before making his pronouncement, "Yup, that's her." Against my will I too look at the waxy, masklike face and catch a glimpse of the body wrapped in its white linen shroud. At first I do not recognize my aunt, but, when I find the familiar shape of her jaw, the other features begin to make more sense.

Later that afternoon, when everyone has left, my father is lying on his bed, fully clothed and covered with a blanket. The room is dark, but he is not asleep. I sit by his side as we review the events of the day. My father, no longer tense and on edge, is philosophical. I am surprised to realize that he wants to talk about his own life, not my aunt's. Once again, he reviews his sense of failure as a businessman and family provider. I remind him that my brother and I had excellent educations, traveled extensively, and never lacked for anything. I remind him too that he has always acted ethically and lovingly, shouldering much of the emotional and physical burden of caring for three of his own siblings. My reminders seem to go unheeded. Then, wistfully and nostalgically, as if out of nowhere, I hear him say, "I had such high hopes for myself, for you boys..."

Now I am lying by my father's side in the darkened room. I am moved to picture him as a young father, dreaming and planning for his "boys." I wonder if Dr. M heard the same innocence and sadness in his voice during the very years that these hopes first came to life. I am also moved to wonder how my father can see my brother and me as disappointments. I recall his injunction weeks before not to be afraid and to ask anything I need to know. I summon all my courage to ask the riskiest question of my life: "And did we, Dad? Did we at least fulfill some of your expectations?" He pauses momentarily, then murmurs softly and sweetly, "Oh yes, oh yes."

For the moment, my father has forgotten, if not forgiven, himself, and he is ready to rest, if not sleep. I slip away from his side, grateful for his ultimate words of approval.

Coda

If I am not for myself, who will be for me?
If I am not for others, what am I?
If not now, when?

HILLEL

I first began to write the bits and pieces of narrative that were to become this book as a way to keep my head above water. I was swamped
by the needs of my two fiercely independent parents who were no
longer able to manage on their own. Frustrated and impatient, I often
felt myself hurled back to a past that I had worked so diligently to
escape from. There were also moments when, with a cooler eye, I was
intrigued by this new stage in my parents' lives and my own. I started
asking unsettling and ultimately unanswerable questions about how
well I knew my parents and understood my childhood. Seeing them
from the vantage point of fifty, now sixty, I learned to read childhood
itself as an unfinished book, one that is open to constant revision as
circumstances change and time erodes the certainties that we attempt
to build our adult lives on.

At the start I imagined a book that would tell the story of the
difficult transitional years when my parents moved from being elderly
and self-sufficient to being elderly and totally reliant on others. A
book about a late-life transition seemed challenging but not impossi-

ble, an opportunity to explore a critical turning point that so many of my peers were helping their own parents to navigate. As an early childhood educator, I knew that transitions are frequently stressful times when people do the double work of mourning the loss of familiar places and people and of anxiously anticipating the unknowns that lie ahead. I wanted to use these insights to describe my parents' life and my role in it.

I even convinced myself that I could tell a story of decline and disintegration while avoiding a final deathbed scene. My parents had reached a plateau, and surely the end itself would not be as difficult as the preceding years. Unconsciously, I assumed they would go on forever.

As a primary caregiver, I live for many years in dread of the late night phone call—the hospital nurse alerting me to a precipitous drop in vital signs, one parent calling because the other has collapsed and refuses to go to the hospital, a home attendant reporting that she cannot come to work the next day. On the night of July 16, 2002, I go to bed with an additional, if unnamable, anxiety. Bob is traveling on assignment, photographing women who have received small grants from a private foundation that supports a wide range of projects to benefit other women. Earlier in the afternoon Deborah Light, the head of the foundation, calls to say that one of the grantees in Green Bay, Wisconsin, has notified her about canceling an appointment for the following day. Deborah has tried unsuccessfully to contact Bob. Have I spoken with him? When Bob travels we talk almost daily, but we hadn't that morning. When I phone the Green Bay hotel myself I learn that he has neither checked in nor canceled his reservation. Bob is conscientious to a fault, so this is unusual behavior for him, but I decide to put it out of my mind. What else can I do? Surely he will call first thing in the morning. The vicissitudes of travel have undoubtedly sent him to another hotel or straight on to Chicago.

The call comes at 12:45 AM. Police detectives bring the news of Bob's sudden and completely unexpected death. At first they don't want to say anything unless they can speak with Bob's wife or parents. Increasingly frightened by the suspicions of foul play that gay men of a certain age so immediately accede to, I demand directness: "If you have anything to say, say it to me, and say it now. I am Bob's life partner." Confronted with my assertion of emotional authority, their legal defenses give way. Bob is dead. A "cardiovascular event" has killed him while he was traveling between Green Bay, Wisconsin, and Chicago. No one on the public bus notices anything strange but the driver is unable to rouse him once they reach the terminal. He has died without a sound, without a motion, and without anyone's knowledge.

Despite the authority I summon up that night, there are many conversations over the succeeding weeks in which I feel powerless and vulnerable. My right to make decisions is questioned at every turn. After all, there had been no wedding, no commitment ceremony, and no public celebration of any kind to commemorate our relationship. We can't even remember the exact date we met, sometime in the fall of 1971 we reckon when asked.

It's true that over time we amassed the kind of documents that have become increasingly possible—a shared mortgage, bank account, wills, health insurance, domestic partnership agreement. Ultimately none of these will prove sufficient to allow me to sign for the cremation that Bob wanted, nor to sign for what I learn to call the "cremains," an unbearably graceless, dare I say, ugly word that is part of the funeral business in America.

A '60s activist, I don't give in easily. I rally a lawyer in New York, an Illinois Department of Health official, and the funeral homes in two cities to a conference call. Ultimately I am left with the decision to spend weeks in court or allow Bob's sister, Cynthia, to sign the papers that will finally allow for the cremation and the ashes to come home. Over the last several years Cynthia has had her hands full. Sharing a house with Bob's parents, she has become the primary caregiver as they begin to experience multiple health problems. In addition, Bob's younger brother had only recently died after a long and difficult set of illnesses. Now within a year, his parents will have lost two adult children. When I reach her, Cynthia is thoughtful, accommodating, and fast to act as we arrange for her to sign and return the necessary papers. Three years later, however, my outrage is unabated. After thirty years together the law deems me unsuitable to carry out Bob's final wishes. Who might know them better? Whose authority should supersede my own?

Although we do not have the documents that would prove valid across state lines, we did possess a deeply satisfying relationship that offers the emotional comforts and practical supports necessary to productive adult lives. With Bob's death, I lose my bearings. Daily events no longer have meaning and bigger existential questions are unapproachable.

I miss Bob in the myriad ways that living and working together for thirty years in the same small house makes inevitable. At the same time, I am surprised to find that from the first I am able to do certain kinds of work. That summer, as a close friend stands guard over the front door, turning away visitors wishing to extend their sympathies, I complete my course syllabus, send out two conference proposals, and edit a paper for publication. Only now however, three years later, have I been able to return to the intensely autobiographical and highly theoretical essays that have characterized my scholarship over the last twenty years.

Soon after that first fall semester begins, I see an old colleague and friend in the hallway at the graduate school where I teach. She has written to me over the summer but this is our first meeting. Perhaps because of our history, and because her own husband had died only recently, it is easy for her to read my face, filled as it is with discomfort and all the concerns for my own viability brought on by such an unanticipated loss. We stand there awkwardly. As she struggles to find words of consolation, I remind her of how, only weeks after her husband's death, she had so graciously given out diplomas at the graduation ceremonies. She admits that she, too, is amazed when she looks back at pictures of that day. It was the students' time, their moment to be recognized for the achievement that graduation signaled. In her slow, thoughtful manner she summarizes, "Over time, I think it is different, not easier. It never really gets better." Finally, she adds, "You do what is necessary."

Through the rollercoaster ride since Bob's death, the ambush of surprising emotions that continues to meet me at every turn, these words remain a reassuring touchstone. I certainly feel that I am doing the necessary as I head to New York City a week after Bob's death, even before the "cremains" are actually returned, let alone the clothing, cameras, and papers that he traveled with, everything identified with its own bright orange tag connected by old-fashioned copper wire—ROBERT GIARD; 172; CASE NO. 319; JUL 02. My destination is the office of one of our oldest friends, a lawyer. As a gay man I am keyed to the potential for mishap, for interventions from long-silent family members who may contest a will or make a claim despite all the legal documents that should make such events impossible. I have only to think back to the scene in the lawyer's office that opens this book and the manner in which my parents had essentially, if unintentionally, written me out of their wills, to know that I am doing what is necessary to protect myself and to protect Bob's work. I have no reason to suspect any untoward interference from Bob's family. I just want to make sure that everything is in order. That's what gay people with a sense of history do.

I go to this meeting alone, my backpack filled with various legal papers along with a list of questions. I eschew the offers of close friends to accompany me. I am still running on overdrive, plowing ahead, numb but in charge. The meeting occurs without incident and the estate specialist who my friend has asked to join us is clear about what needs to be done. Nevertheless, when I walk out of that law office and onto Fifth Avenue, something has changed. I feel weak and hollow, as if I might be blown over by the slightest wind on that breezeless July day.

For one thing, I know that I can no longer manage alone. Until this time, friends in my neighborhood visit each day. They take turns answering the endless telephone calls, bringing food, helping to make decisions. They return home at night. Suddenly that will not be enough. I walk for a while until I find a public phone, no small achievement in the age of cellular phones and e-mail. I call my cousin and ask her to come to Amagansett. It is Wednesday and she can be there by Friday. "Would that be OK?" she asks. "No," I reply. Can she arrive by tomorrow afternoon when Bob's obituary is scheduled to appear in the local paper? It will undoubtedly prompt more calls from which I want to be protected. For the first time in the week since Bob's death, I feel that I am falling apart, a full-scale meltdown is in progress. My cousin's commitment to Thursday secured, I call an old friend whose initial suggestion of a visit I had rejected. Now I am ready and she will need to be there as soon as my cousin leaves. I am constructing a human fence tough enough to protect me, porous enough to mediate the world when required, and malleable enough to support my baffling moods and emotions.

Then I inexplicably find myself on the subway heading uptown toward my father's nursing home. My niece has taken responsibility for informing my mother about Bob but I know that no one has spoken with my father. While my mother, accompanied by her health aide, visits him daily, winding her way through the two lines of wheelchairs that are often to be found outside his door for the postlunch change of scene, their attempts at communication are often botched. Both suffer from hearing and vision loss. She cannot read his finely printed words. He cannot hear her comments. More importantly, the ministrokes, which she has endured without major damage, have left her with minor cognitive deficits. She does not have the flexibility to adjust to my father's many moods. Of course, she knows when he is depressed, angry, or out of control but is unable to see subtle difference or to modify her own responses accordingly. To me, it seems that my mother is neither able to give my father what he needs nor to get back anything to sustain her own fragile life. Nevertheless she goes every day. When snowstorms make travel hazardous she sends her health aide as her ambassador. She cannot tolerate the idea that my father might pass one day without seeing a member of the family and thus feel abandoned. It takes many months to convince my mother that a "day off" to keep a medical appointment is not a disloyal or unloving act.

Truth be told, because my father slips so easily between manic and depressive states and suffers from prolonged periods of dementia, it is often hard to know what to expect upon entering his room. At times he is not even in the room but out in the hallway frantically writing notes and wildly gesticulating about the staff's refusal to take him to the development office so that he can give the nursing home a million-dollar gift. On other days, he schemes about installing two telephones, one on either side of his bed, even though he is voiceless and unable to carry on a conversation. On yet other days he is absorbed by some small affront or failure of the staff to respond quickly enough to his request for suctioning. Most offensive is their insistence that he get out of the bed for a few hours each day, which he feels is too great an effort.

Going to visit my father is a journey for which I pack carefully. Beyond a great deal of protective gear, I try to manage something diverting as well. On some days I bring old family photos. At first blush, what might appear to be severe dementia will then give way to a few minutes of focused attention. When I thrust the pictures in front of my father, he can identify everyone, including himself at age five, standing alone in front of the family home in Erie, Pennsylvania, dressed in an English-style winter coat with velvet collar. Occasionally the photos lead to family stories; mostly they end with a simpler labeling project. I am never sure how much he can comprehend. Several weeks after viewing the picture of himself at five, for example, I watch my father write the barber, whose prior attempts to trim his now long hair he graciously but forcefully resists, that he would be pleased if she could cut his hair, "in the manner of a small boy."

On another day, in desperation to end a tantrum about the telephone lines, I pull my recently published book from my backpack. He takes it from my hands, examines it slowly and carefully, and then writes, "Is it only published in paperback? No hard cover?" Rebuke, sincere inquiry, subtle put-down? I respond with laughter, naming his return to this world, and speak for a few minutes about the contents of the book before he drifts off to sleep.

Surely he is pleased, however, the day I come to his room directly after giving a talk a few blocks north at Columbia University. Then I report reading a narrative about his love of language. He smiles appreciatively but expresses no desire to read it himself. While nursing home residents often imagine that they are temporarily staying in a hotel, my father, ever the intellectual, sometimes believes that he is living in a university, the psychologists and psychiatrists who test him part of the faculty who simply enjoy his company.

I have no idea how my father will respond to the news I carry in my backpack that July afternoon three years ago. Walking across 112th Street in Manhattan, I rely on my experiences with HIV/AIDS. I remember how it feels when impelled to do things for myself, not necessarily for the person who is sick—a cross-country visit to someone in a coma, a phone call to someone else with dementia, so many words spoken that cannot possibly be understood. I never regret these actions, but neither am I confused about their purpose. As on this day, I act out of my own needs, not anticipating a response from the other. I feel that no matter my father's emotional state, telling him about Bob's death is the only respectful thing to do, the only way to acknowledge that he still matters to me and is part of the world. Despite all his erratic behavior, there is an ethical and emotional imperative that draws me toward him. And I am not to be disappointed.

When I arrive he is calm, and after some banter about his latest discontents, I tell him why I have come. He listens carefully but does not respond. As with young children, I reframe my comments and use other words to make clear that he will never see Bob again. I try to check for his comprehension—no written response, no change of facial expression. I decide to drop the subject. After all, I am not there for his sympathy. We sit quietly together and he peruses the newspaper. Then it is time for me to go, my mission accomplished. We are not an openly affectionate family, hugging and kissing not part of our usual comings and goings. My father is sitting in his wheelchair and as I lean down to look him in the eye and say goodbye, he reaches up with his bony, arthritic hands and pulls me toward him, planting a deep kiss on my forehead. Then I know he understands.

In the following weeks I am preoccupied with securing Bob's ashes from the funeral home in Chicago and his possessions from the police department, and finally organizing a memorial service. I do not get to New York City nor is my mother mobile enough to come to the service. The afternoon before the memorial my father writes to my mother, "If the service for Bob is tomorrow, could you call Jonathan for me." I am amazed that he knows the exact day of the memorial. My mother's approach is to avoid bringing up such subjects. Of course, she follows his instructions. I am moved by his attention then and even more on my next visit when I find these words on his pad, "It was a sad day for me when I realized that Bob was gone." What more could a gay son want from his father? So close to the end of his own life, what more does he possibly have to give?

My return to work that fall after Bob's death is not easy. At the end of the semester, a few students write in their course evaluations that I am distant and unapproachable. Those comments surprise one of my colleagues, who reads them as she prepares for my annual review. Her own experience with me has been very different, involving many lively conversations about our work. She asks me if I have told my students about my partner's death. When I say that I carefully considered this possibility and decided not to, she wonders aloud if the students' comments might reflect that decision.

Despite the many unconventional aspects of my pedagogy—speaking openly about being a gay man working with young children, requiring students to write personal narratives, engaging with postmodern theory, and conducting conversations about controversial subjects with children—I do not want to talk with my students about Bob's death. I worry that such a disclosure will place an undue burden on them—students whom I don't know well and many of whom are struggling to become adults. Would a perception of my vulnerability affect their ability to challenge me and test their ideas against my own? I am not willing to risk becoming another person for whom they will need to care, nor do I trust my ability to handle the complex emotions that such an announcement might evoke in my students or in me.

Slowly, however, I begin to question this self-imposed silence. I am committed to transparency as an essential way of prompting students to examine their assumptions about teaching and learning. I ask them to consider how sharing particular information, life experiences, and ways of thinking might help them understand themselves better, or expand their own students' horizons. Needless to say, I ask the same questions of myself.

With respect to Bob's death and its implications for who I am as a teacher, I do not have very good answers yet. For two years, not talking about his death may have been the way that life-altering event entered my pedagogy. An open exploration of moments when teachers and students choose to remain silent, a topic that I am newly curious about, may help my own students to understand that profound loss is almost always part of the classroom, whether acknowledged or not.

Then something happens that gives me the chance to move through the silence. It is the night that I invite Lenore Furman to talk about the "News of the Day" book she writes in her kindergarten classroom. Before group meeting each morning, children have a chance to dictate an event that has occurred outside of school. Lenore brings a sample book to our class as well as a video of an especially memorable day.

Keisha's mom is eight months pregnant and everyone is waiting excitedly, if somewhat impatiently, for the birth of Keisha's first sibling. Then, after missing several days of school, Keisha comes back. She sits down quietly next to Lenore. Invited to add something to the News of the Day book, Keisha carefully tells this story: "My mom had went to the hospital and she had her baby and it died. It was born too early. My mommy was crying."

When the group gathers on the rug, Lenore asks the children who have contributed that morning if she can read their News of the Day out loud. Keisha sits next to Lenore again and is indeed eager to have her news read. When asked if there is anything she wants to add, she says "no." Lenore herself then reviews the basics of pregnancy and childbirth that have been part of the ongoing curriculum. She reassures the children that only in rare circumstances do babies die. The class listens quietly and closely to everything that Lenore says.

In succeeding weeks Keisha's entries return to the theme of loss: "My hamster died. They were fighting." "My fish died and my bird died." "I thought I lost the book but my mommy found it on the hamster cage."

My students have many questions. How does Lenore manage with twenty-seven children? How did she respond to Keisha when she first heard her story? What kind of administrative support does she have for these difficult conversations?

When Lenore leaves, Suzanne comments that she was struck by the silence of the other children in the classroom when Keisha's news was read. As Suzanne speaks and others respond, I thought back to my experience just after Bob died. Upon returning to work, I wanted people to know but it was too soon for conversations of any sort. So with the help of a close friend I crafted a brief response to acknowledge the sympathy expressed by colleagues and to make clear that I would not engage in talk about the topic.

Feeling uneasy yet determined, I tell the class my own story and how it influences my reading of Keisha's behavior. As they say, you could hear a pin drop in our room.

Then Dan breaks the silence. He recounts the time that Steven, one of his first graders, told the class about the death of his grandmother. Dan notes that other students responded by offering their own stories of loss but did not speak directly to Steven. Dan felt disappointed by this conversation. He describes the children as egocentric. I, on the other hand, see the long shadow still cast by Piaget in Dan's words, a shadow that always underestimates children's cognitive and emotional lives. For me, despite the absence of direct expressions of sympathy, the children's counter-stories are best interpreted as attempts to identify and empathize with Steven.

Again, there is another long pause in our own conversation. The silence is palpable. Taking what feels like a further risk, I speak about the many losses endured by my colleagues in recent years. My instinct is to listen when someone wants to talk and, now that I am ready, to answer with my own experience. I am unable to imagine what it is like for Jeannie to lose her husband, Katherine her life partner, or Ken his father. Perhaps, not unlike Dan's students, I reach out by sharing my own life.

As our conversation winds down that night, I wonder what my students understand about my own stories of managing loss. I remember that earlier in the semester, Deanna said she would not read a children's book about a homeless family because she did not want to cry in front of her class. Like others in our group, she felt that children could not tolerate seeing adult expressions of vulnerability. Do my students need the same kind of protection? Have I gone too far?

Considering Suzanne's concerns and my own, I ask the group if my stories have made me vulnerable in their eyes. Have I lost authority when talking about Bob's death?

As a teacher educator, I feel responsible for making my pedagogy visible and legible, no matter how discomforting that might be. If I want my students to take risks in their classrooms, don't I have to do the same? That night we leave thoughtfully and quietly. Something has changed for all of us. Our class of eighteen individuals is definitely becoming a group. We are working hard to understand how authentic learning occurs in the classroom.

Distracted by Bob's death, my ability to care for my parents is severely compromised. That first December my brother and I decide to move my mother from the large apartment where we grew up and which she has lived in for nearly fifty years into her sister's even larger apartment. There is no other choice but a nursing home. Neither alternative is acceptable to my mother. Unfortunately, my parents have long ago run out of money and there are limits to my brother's resources, which have sustained them for several years. My mother is in a state of despair. Life as she knows it is coming to end. Her grief is deep and all too real.

Although I try to encourage my mother's participation in selecting the furniture and few small objects she will take with her, she is paralyzed. I insist that the apartment remain completely intact until she walks out the front door. The chaos on the inside is not to be mirrored by disorder on the outside. Here I am undoubtedly speaking for myself as well. I cannot tolerate yet another disruption in the world I have known. I am ready to reconstruct a new home for my mother but not to dismantle the old. I leave that task to other family members.

Having heard endless accounts from friends of ugly family squabbles about the division of property, I arrange to go through my parents' apartment with my niece on an afternoon when my mother is at the nursing home. Anne and I have always worked well together and she is empowered to speak for her parents. I understand that the vase that stood for so long on the entryway table and filled weekly with fresh flowers, the set of china handed down from a favorite grandmother and only used on special occasions, and even the jewelry that made my mother appear so elegant on rare nights out, will soon end up out of sight, stored away in boxes. With this knowledge in mind, dividing up the furniture and other objects of monetary or sentimental value proceeds easily. We alternate choices, make concessions, note our sometimes different, sometimes similar sense of aesthetics, all while sharing stories elicited by the task at hand.

Fortunately, when my mother sees her familiar possessions assembled in her new room she is genuinely pleased. It is an auspicious beginning for what turns out to be the best possible compromise for all concerned. My aunt, at ninety-two, two years older than my mother, is in the early stages of Alzheimer's. Her initial worries about the loss of privacy that could happen with the new living arrangements do not materialize. Her own life is becoming increasingly circumscribed and self-absorbed. The sisters, each with her own caregiver, seem to genuinely enjoy each other's company, and benefit from the distractions provided by the other's visitors. My aunt, more outgoing, more able to confront life's vicissitudes, more willing to see the positive, shares with my mother not only a ninety-year history but also a propensity for critique of the caregivers to whom they are both in reality closely attached. It is as if this dinnertime ritual of criticism draws them together for a few minutes each night, an act of resistance to their dependency as well as an evocation of an era gone by.

While not her choice, my mother's move was fortunate in other ways that could not have been predicted at the time. In March, after several bouts of pneumonia, my father suddenly dies. Already ensconced in her sister's apartment, my mother has ready-made company and cannot sink into complete despair. I do not think she would have tolerated the death of my father and the loss of familiar surroundings had one followed immediately upon the other.

I am not with my father when he dies. I visit him several days before, prompted by a call from the nursing home. Going through the giant blue binder that contains his most recent medical history, the floor nurse cannot find a "do not resuscitate" (DNR) order on file. Would I please fill one out or speak with my father about it?

In the late morning of a fine March day I walk from my office to my father's room in the nursing home. He is most alert and at his best before lunch, and my mother will not yet have arrived, a potentially complicating factor. I find him surprisingly calm and relaxed. It seems as if the bouts of pneumonia that he suffered from all winter have drained him of the dementia and extreme mood swings. I stand close by his bedside so he can see me with his good eye and hear me clearly. After two pairs of hearing aids disappear, we do not bother with a third. They are simply too small or too valuable to be tracked by the nursing home staff. I explain the reason for my visit. My father looks at me with understanding and replies in his increasingly weak but still legible print, "Of course I want a DNR order. I've always wanted one." His tone is almost indignant. How could his wishes have not been known and carried out? "OK, Dad," I reply with great relief, no longer put off by his minor assertions of authority. "Do you want to sign it yourself or should I?" His response, "You sign it," is both a dismissive command and an indication of trust. Nothing is ever simple.

After I take care of the paperwork, I return to spend an unusually easy hour with my father. One topic leads comfortably into the next. As I walk back to my office I am thankful for the satisfying interview. The clarity and crispness of the day echoes the mood in my father's room. I know it's been a special time but not exactly how special until several days later.

Again it is the floor nurse who calls in late afternoon to say that the nursing home is sending my father to the hospital emergency room. They have been trying unsuccessfully over the past week to get him an appointment with a pulmonologist and have determined on the emergency room strategy as the fastest way to get him evaluated. I know this unhappy strategy only too well and that my father might be stranded in a hospital corridor for many hours waiting to be seen. Partially blind, his writing now deteriorated so that it is almost impossible for strangers to read, he may be forced to lie on a gurney unable to communicate. The nurse assures me that of course they will send his chart with him, but it is against policy to send a human being. It is not a life-threatening situation. Then why not wait until the morning, when it is more feasible for him to be accompanied by a family member? Is the situation more serious than she is willing to let on? How hard has the home really tried for the pulmonologist's assessment in the preceding weeks? Is this simply bad timing, or a lack of forethought?

I have just returned to Amagansett from New York and immediately call my brother, who happens to be in the city. He is reluctant to leave his business meeting. I explain in graphic detail what my father's experience is likely to be in the emergency room. Within the hour my brother calls from the hospital, where he has been able to locate my father. No doctor has examined him yet. An hour later there is another call. A doctor has just seen my father and diagnosed him with sepsis, a severe and often fatal infection. My brother reports that even though they have started him on massive doses of antibiotics, in the doctor's words, "the prognosis isn't good." I am in shock. From a pulmonary assessment to a deadly infection? When did it begin? Before he got to the hospital? In the emergency room itself, a function of a severely compromised immune system? Of course my brother can't answer these questions, nor can I convince him to stay any longer. It's close to 7 PM. I get the doctor's phone number and am surprised to reach her immediately. Yes, she has seen my father. I push for a definitive statement about the "bad prognosis." She is friendly and professional but resists my prodding. Finally hearing my insistence, she uses guarded, carefully chosen words to tell me that "in cases like your father's, if he doesn't respond to the drugs within two or three hours, he may not last the night."

By now I've missed the last bus to New York and I don't trust myself alone on the long drive. Perhaps more to the point, I am not impelled to be with my father. I believe that our "final" moment has occurred earlier in the week, when he directed me to sign the DNR order. He was calm, in charge, almost heroic during that encounter and there is part of me that wants to remember him that way. There is part of me too that is exhausted by the years filled with all of the unheroic moments when his needs took precedence over everyone else's. In what turns out to be this final night of my father's life, I am paralyzed by the inevitability of another loss only eight months after Bob's death. I keep my physical distance because I need to sustain an emotional barrier. In this way I am selfish and self-protective. These are hardly admirable emotions, hardly the thoughts of an ideal caregiver, but all too real nonetheless.

I want someone to be with my father and in my eyes that person should be my brother. I call my brother at home and tell him what the doctor has said. He does not believe that my father recognizes him any longer and sees no reason to go back to the hospital. The one thing we agree upon is not to call my mother, who seems too frail to withstand an all-night bedside vigil. At 11:00 PM my brother calls from my father's room. He has enlisted Anne to accompany him. The drugs have not taken effect and my father mostly sleeps. Why stay?

The next day I learn that my brother and Anne wait for a while longer and then, when asked to leave the room for a few minutes while the nurses try to make my father more comfortable, leave. My father dies alone somewhere between 3 and 4 AM. I am not surprised by the 5 AM call with the news. It's not like the call about Bob's death. I experience no disbelief and very little emotion at all other than relief that his interminable suffering has ended and that we have managed a successful final interview. I do wonder, why now? Why not two years ago or two weeks from now? The moment of death is completely arbitrary.

In the months to follow I forgive myself as I know my father would have forgiven me for being an imperfect caregiver, for not rushing to his beside in the middle of the night. More disquieting is the unexpected guilt that I experience when thinking about my father's death at all. I am torn between two losses and believe that all my emotional attention rightfully belongs to Bob. Yet images of my father periodically intrude into the carefully measured spaces that I have created to contemplate my life with and now without Bob. It's an awkward, unsettling internal competition, one that neither Bob nor my father would approve, one that I hope is ended in these pages, in this attempt to make sense of the final years of my father's life.

I am not a spiritual person, but I am convinced that my father knew in his last weeks that the end was near and that he was prepared as best he could be. He did not leave us money and property, as he had dreamed in his younger days. Nor did he leave a public record of accomplishments that can be recognized by others, something that he hoped his children might achieve. In the last months of his life, however, my father did give me rare, profoundly moving moments of recognition. These moments, many mediated by Bob's death, do not make up for his demanding and controlling ways that permeated much of my life. They do offer a sense of a circle completed, a life well lived, and a final set of instructions on what it means to be a caregiver to the very end.

Acknowledgments

Nineteenth-century images of Romantic authors writing alone in their rooms, channeling the artistic muse, still cast their long shadow over the twenty-first century. Most books more accurately reflect the complex ways that our lives are bound up with others. They are the products of socially constructed worlds as much as, if not more than, solitary, interior reflection. The acknowledgments that follow—and I apologize in advance to those whom I may have inadvertently failed to mention—attest to the collaborative nature of authorship, even of memoir.

Many members of my chosen family helped to make life tolerable in the face of intolerable losses and understood that for better or worse, my life and my work were inextricably tied together. Thank you—Chelsea Bailey and Marshall Weber, Gail Boldt, Muriel Dimen, Allen Ellenzweig, James and John Haigney, Michael Hampton and Carlos Sandoval, Cindy Jurow, Dolores Klaich, Barry and Arlene Klingman, Michael Piore and Rodney Yoder, Eric Rofes, Erika Shank, Glenn Stancroff, Toba Tucker, and Karen Weiss. I gratefully acknowledge too the support of my Bank Street family, past and present —Nancy Balaban, Virginia Casper, Harriet Cuffaro, Lia Gelb, Nancy Gropper, Judy Leipzig, Carol Lippman, Mimi Rosenberg, and Edna Shapiro.

Members of my given family have contributed each in his or her own way to sustaining my parents. My brother, Robert, generously provided the resources necessary to keep my father out of an institution for as long as was possible and insured that my mother never entered one. Anne, my niece and coconspirator in the work of eldercare, always kept me on my toes, asking questions that reminded me of the multiple perspectives that our lives may be viewed from. I am deeply indebted as well to the emotional and practical generosity of my cousins—Jill Prosky and James Posner—without whom my mother's final years would have been very different indeed. I am thankful too for my mother's rare moments of laughter and good humor, which punctuated the hard times, and my aunt's courage and wisdom in the face of adversity, which I can only hope to emulate.

I will never forget the professional caregivers—Yvonne Calvin, Marlene Eubanks, and Sandra Mundy—who so conscientiously looked after my father at home. Despite the many trying moments, they all appreciated his humor, determination to control as much of his life as possible, and ultimate will to survive.

A minigrant from Bank Street College of Education supported initial work on this project. The East End Writers' Group offered sage critique of the early essays. Other colleagues willingly and insightfully read drafts of the manuscript—Wendy Fairey, Judith Levine, Jo Anne Pagano, Fran Schwartz, and Peter Taubman. My thanks as well to Bill Ayers, who always remembers and isn't shy. Without the astute and caring stewardship of Helene Atwan, director of Beacon Press, the book would not have seen the light of day.

In the end it was Bob Giard, my partner of thirty years, who made work on this project possible. For it was Bob who taught me how to love and how to forgive, when to fight fiercely and when to let go. Above all he understood that it is in the smallest acts of human kindness that we often reveal our deepest feelings and our profoundest respect for human life. It is hard to imagine entering the country of the frail elderly without him.